I AND 2 TIMOTHY, TITUS, PHILEMON

H. A. IRONSIDE

I AND 2 TIMOTHY, TITUS, PHILEMON

An Ironside Expository Commentary

H. A. Ironside

KREGEL
MINISTRY

1 and 2 Timothy, Titus, and Philemon: An Ironside Expository Commentary
by H. A. Ironside

Originally published in 1947. Reprinted in 2008 by Kregel Publications, a division of Kregel Inc., 2450 Oak Industrial Dr. NE, Grand Rapids, MI 49505.

Unless otherwise noted, Scripture quotations are from the King James Version of the Holy Bible.

Scripture quotations marked RV are from the Revised Version of the Holy Bible (Church of England, 1885).

ISBN 978-0-8254-4260-5

Printed in the United States of America

Contents

Part 1: 1 Timothy

Part 2: 2 Timothy

PART 1

1 Timothy

CHAPTER 1

INTRODUCTION

1 Timothy 1:1–4

> Paul, an apostle of Jesus Christ by the commandment of God our Saviour, and Lord Jesus Christ, which is our hope; unto Timothy, my own son in the faith: Grace, mercy, and peace, from God our Father and Jesus Christ our Lord. As I besought thee to abide still at Ephesus, when I went into Macedonia, that thou mightest charge some that they teach no other doctrine, neither give heed to fables and endless genealogies, which minister questions, rather than godly edifying which is in faith: so do. (vv. 1–4)

There are three letters of Paul that we generally speak of as Pastoral Epistles: 1 and 2 Timothy, and Titus. They are so-called because they were written to servants of Christ who, in a very special sense, had the care of God's people in different places. These two young men had been converted through the instrumentality of the apostle Paul and had gone out to preach the Word in association with him. From time to time he left one or the other to help in various newly formed churches in order that the young converts might be established in the truth. Both of these young men had shepherds' hearts and delighted to care for the sheep and lambs of Christ's flock. In these three letters Paul writes to them regarding certain things which, as pastors, or shepherds of the flock, they needed to keep in mind. Of course, these letters are not only for those who have special gifts along these lines, but they also contain instruction for all God's people.

The great outstanding theme of the two epistles to Timothy is "the truth according to godliness," while that of the letter to Titus is "godliness according to truth," thus giving us the two sides of the subject. In the letters to Timothy, Paul emphasizes the importance of holding fast the faithful Word; in that to Titus he stresses the necessity of godly living in accordance with the Word of truth.

The first letter to Timothy was evidently written after Paul's release from his first imprisonment; therefore, it is a later letter than the Prison Epistles, such as Philippians, Colossians, Ephesians, and some others. First Timothy was written after Paul had appeared before Caesar. Because the charges against him were not found sufficient to warrant his execution, Paul was set free. If we can trust the records that have come down from the early days, Paul then went as far west as Spain, preaching the Word. He returned later to the East and ministered throughout Asia Minor, different parts of Greece, and Macedonia. After several years he was rearrested and taken back to Rome, and on this second occasion was condemned to death. First Timothy fits in between his liberation and the second arrest, while the second letter to Timothy was written from Paul's death cell.

This first letter seems to divide into five parts: chapter 1 is the first division, and the outstanding theme is grace contrasted with law. Chapter 2, the second division, stresses the importance of prayer, both public and private. Chapter 3 is the third division and gives the divine order in the church of God. Chapter 4, the fourth division, is a prophecy of conditions that will prevail in the latter times, and the importance of holding fast to the truth as apostasy rolls on. Chapters 5 and 6 together give the fifth division of the book in which we have various admonitions not only for Timothy but also for all of us.

We notice at this time just the four opening verses of the first chapter. In the first two verses we have the apostolic salutation: "Paul, an apostle of Jesus Christ by the commandment of God our Saviour, and Lord Jesus Christ, which is our hope; unto Timothy, my own son in the faith: Grace, mercy, and peace, from God our Father and Jesus Christ our Lord." An apostle is a "sent one." The meaning is almost the same as that of our word *missionary,* but the word *missionary* does not necessarily carry with it a sense of authority. The apostles were appointed by the Lord Jesus Christ, specially commissioned and sent forth to proclaim His gospel throughout the world. We have twelve apostles in the Gospels. Judas forfeited his place by his treachery. In the first chapter of Acts we have Matthias elected to fill the place of Judas, and that makes the Twelve complete.

The apostleship of Paul was of an altogether different order. The Lord Jesus said to the Twelve that in the regeneration, that is, in the coming glorious kingdom, "Ye which have followed me, in the regeneration when the Son of man shall sit in the throne of his glory, ye also shall sit upon twelve thrones, judging the twelve tribes of Israel" (Matt. 19:28). Paul could not be included in that list because he did not know the Lord during His life on earth. But Matthias was one who had kept company with the apostles from the days of John the Baptist until the time of his election to fill the place of Judas (Acts 1:21–22). Evidently it was by the Spirit's guidance that he was elected to fill that place.

God had a special ministry for the apostle Paul: he was to make known the truth of the mystery of the body of Christ, and was commissioned to go unto the Gentiles and proclaim the glorious message of the gospel in all its power and fullness. He had special authority committed unto him as an apostle of Jesus Christ, "By the commandment," he says, "of God our Saviour, and Lord Jesus Christ, which is our hope."

I like that expression: "God our Savior." Many are inclined to think of God as a Judge rather than as a Savior; but remember, it was God who "so loved the world, that he gave his only begotten Son, that whosoever believeth in him should not perish, but have everlasting life" (John 3:16). The death of our Lord Jesus Christ on the cross did not enable God to love men. It was the expression of the love of God toward men. "Herein is love, not that we loved God, but that he loved us, and sent his Son to be the propitiation for our sins" (1 John 4:10). And so now we who are saved can look up to Him and say, "God our Savior!" Ordinarily we think of applying this expression to our Lord Jesus Christ. Of course it is more often used in connection with Him than with any other Person of the Godhead, but it is blessedly true that God the Father is our Savior as truly as God the Son. So Paul here links the two together: "God our Saviour, and Lord Jesus Christ, which is our hope." He gives Him His full title.

I wonder if you have ever noticed that when our blessed Lord was here on earth no friend of His is ever said to have addressed Him by His given name, Jesus. That is a lovely name. It is so significant. To many of us it is the sweetest name we have ever heard. It means "Jehovah the Savior." It was the name given to Him in His humanity. But we never read of anyone going up to Him and saying, "Jesus." He was always addressed as Lord or Master, and He approved of that, for He said, "Ye call me Master and Lord: and ye say well; for so I am" (John 13:13). After His death, and inspired by the Spirit of God, the apostles used the simple name "Jesus" very frequently in telling of events that had taken place. But when they wanted to give Him special honor they used His full title—the Lord Jesus Christ. He is Lord because He should have absolute authority over the hearts of men. He is Jesus because He was Jehovah come down to earth, taking our humanity upon Himself in order that He might save us. As to His office, He is Christ, which means the "Anointed," the "Messiah." Peter said, "God hath made the same Jesus, whom ye have crucified, both Lord and Christ" (Acts 2:36).

"God our Saviour, and Lord Jesus Christ, which is our hope." Christianity has a message of hope. As we look around over the world today we see so many things that have a tendency to make one utterly hopeless and pessimistic. But when we turn to the Word of God we find what He has revealed concerning the present age and the final blessing of this world, and the heart is filled with hope, joy, and comfort. The apostle Paul delighted in that word *hope.* I think you will find it forty times in his epistles. Here it is "the Lord Jesus Christ, which is our hope." In Titus 2:13 we read of "looking for that blessed hope, and the glorious appearing of the great God and our Saviour Jesus Christ." In 1 Thessalonians 1:3 it is "patience of hope in our Lord Jesus Christ, in the sight of God and our Father," and in many other places and ways the apostle uses this word *hope.* The Lord Jesus Christ Himself is our hope. We are looking for Him to return. We are looking for Him to transform these bodies of our humiliation and make them like unto His glorious body. Our hope is to see Him as He is and to become like Him. What a blessed hope it is!

Paul addresses himself to Timothy and speaks of him as "my own son." He really uses the more intimate term in the original, "my own *child* in the faith." In what sense was Timothy his child in the faith? Well, you remember that when the apostle Paul went to Lystra, as recorded in the book of Acts (chap. 14), he was first welcomed as a god and then stoned, as the people thought, to death. But as a result of his ministry at Lystra, a young man, half-Jew and half-Gentile (his mother was Jewish, and his father was a Greek), was brought to a saving knowledge of the Lord Jesus Christ—this young man was Timothy. He had been well-instructed in the Old Testament, and when Paul came to Lystra and preached the gospel Timothy was ready to receive Christ. When Paul went to Lystra the second time some years afterward, the brethren recommended Timothy as one suitable to be set apart for the gospel. Paul had an interview with young Timothy and decided to take him along with him. There were no theological seminaries where people could go for a quick training in spiritual truths and practical work, but the older took the younger with him. Barnabas took Mark with him in early days, and later Mark became the companion of Peter. Paul took different ones with him on various occasions, Timothy, Titus,

Silas, and others. In this way the younger men gained experience and confidence until they were able to launch out independently for the Lord.

Paul had a deep affection for Timothy. There is always a close bond between a servant of Christ and those whom he has led to the Lord as their Savior. I cannot tell you what a joy it is to know that one has been used to bring many to know the Lord Jesus Christ. It just thrills one's heart to think that God has given the privilege of bringing so many with the Spirit's leading to accept Him as their own Redeemer. Oh, there is no joy like this! If you have never led anyone to Christ, and yet you are a Christian, you have missed something that would do your soul good. Try to win someone else to Christ or tell somebody else about the Lord Jesus, and if you have the joy of hearing that person confess Christ as Savior for the first time, you will count it one of the greatest thrills you can have!

Paul's love for Timothy is shown in his words, "My own [child] in the faith." And he wishes him "grace, mercy, and peace." Notice that when he addresses churches or groups of people as such he speaks of "grace and peace," but when addressing an individual he puts in another word, "grace, *mercy,* and peace." Individuals need mercy. Individuals are conscious of their failures; they are conscious of their need of special divine help. In each instance, when Paul speaks to individuals particularly, he gives them this threefold greeting: "Grace, mercy, and peace." It is not the grace that saves in the beginning that he has in view, but the grace that keeps, the grace that sustains: "He giveth more grace" as we go along our pilgrim way. It is not the mercy as a result of which our sins are forgiven in the first place, but that mercy which we need from day to day when conscious of failure and shortcoming, when we come to God and confess our sins: "If we confess our sins, he is faithful and just to forgive us our sins, and to cleanse us from all unrighteousness" (1 John 1:9). It is not the peace *with* God which every believer has—"Being justified by faith, we have peace with God through our Lord Jesus Christ" (Rom. 5:1), we should all enjoy that peace from the very beginning—but here it is the peace *of* God, that peace which keeps our hearts in confidence and restful quietness in the midst of adverse circumstances.

As we read in Philippians 4:6–7, "Be careful [anxious] for nothing; but in every thing by prayer and supplication with thanksgiving let your requests be made known unto God. And the peace of God, which passeth all understanding, shall keep your hearts and minds through Christ Jesus." Did you know that was in the Bible? You have heard it quoted often. You have read it often. But do you practice it? When you get into trouble, what do you do? Do you worry, fret, and say, "Dear me! I do not know how I am going to get through this, or how

I shall face that?" Or do you say to yourself, "God has told me to be anxious about nothing but to tell Him about it"? So you go to Him, spread the whole thing before Him, and say, "It is all right. I know He will undertake. I know He will do what is best."

"Grace, mercy, and peace, from God our Father and Jesus Christ our Lord." God is the Father of all who believe; He is the Creator of all men. But man, who was created in the image and likeness of God, has turned away from Him. Sin came in, and the image was marred and the likeness lost, so men have to be born again. Jesus emphasized that when He said to Nicodemus, "Except a man be born again, he cannot see the kingdom of God" (John 3:3). When men trust Him as Savior, when they believe the message of the gospel, they receive this new life. They are born again. They have a right to look up to God and say, "Father!" Do you know Him as your Father? He is a loving Father. He is deeply interested in every detail of your life. There are many people who have trusted Christ as Savior who, I fear, have never yet realized His Lordship. Beware of calling Jesus "Lord," and slighting His command. There is a little ditty that goes something like this:

If He is not Lord of all,
Then He is not Lord at all.

He should have absolute authority over our lives, for we have been bought with a price, even His precious blood. If you have trusted Him as Savior, then recognize His lordship and give Him the right-of-way in your heart and life.

Now it is evident that the apostle, acting with apostolic authority, commended a special ministry to Timothy, and yet he did not put it on the ground of a command. He said, "I besought thee to abide still at Ephesus." You see, when grace controls the heart, *I command* becomes *I beseech,* so Paul says, "I besought"—I pleaded with you. The Christians in Ephesus needed help and special ministry, and Paul urged Timothy to remain in Ephesus and lead the saints on and give them pastoral care while Paul, himself, went on to Macedonia.

He gave a special commission to Timothy, "That thou mightest charge some that they teach no other doctrine." It is interesting to trace that little word *some* through this epistle. You will find it frequently: "*Some* having swerved have turned aside unto vain jangling" (1:6); "*Some* having put away [a good conscience] concerning faith have made shipwreck" (1:19); "*Some* shall depart from the faith, giving heed to seducing spirits, and doctrines of devils" (4:1); "*Some* are already turned aside after Satan" (5:15); and so on.

There were those who were teaching things contrary to the truth of God; so Paul says to Timothy, "Stay there if you will and help the saints, and warn those teachers of false things, and charge them that they teach no other doctrine than that which has been delivered unto the saints." Just what that false doctrine was we are not told here, but as we read on it seems evident that it is a mixture of Jewish legality and Oriental mysticism, probably that which eventually resulted in that esoteric religious system which had a large influence for the next one hundred years. It was called *Gnosticism.* Do not misunderstand the word, it is not agnosticism but *Gnosticism.*

"Neither give heed to fables [Oriental fables] and endless genealogies [that refers particularly to certain Jewish genealogies], which minister questions, rather than godly edifying which is in faith: so do." Today we still need to beware of systems that do not build up our souls, but instead only serve to get Christians occupied with unprofitable questions. There are some people who delight to argue. John Bunyan has said, "Some love the meat; some love to pick the bones." And you will find people who delight in picking the bones of vital doctrines but get very little nourishment from the truth of God's Word, because, instead of being occupied with Christ, they are occupied with various side issues. Now Timothy was to warn the saints to beware of things like that. That which builds up the people of God is heart occupation with Christ. If we are taken up with Him we will become increasingly like Him.

CHAPTER 2

Law and Grace

1 Timothy 1:5–11

> Now the end of the commandment is charity out of a pure heart, and of a good conscience, and of faith unfeigned: from which some having swerved have turned aside unto vain jangling; desiring to be teachers of the law; understanding neither what they say, nor whereof they affirm. But we know that the law is good, if a man use it lawfully; knowing this, that the law is not made for a righteous man, but for the lawless and disobedient, for the ungodly and for sinners, for unholy and profane, for murderers of fathers and murderers of mothers, for manslayers, for whoremongers, for them that defile themselves with mankind, for menstealers, for liars, for perjured persons, and if there be any other thing that is contrary to sound doctrine; according to the glorious gospel of the blessed God, which was committed to my trust. (vv. 5–11)

In these words the apostle Paul brings out very vividly the difference between two great principles: that of grace, which has been manifested in the cross, and results in love for God and love for our fellow men when we trust that grace; and the principle of law, which demands a righteousness that sinful man can never fully render. We have noticed that one of the objects which the apostle had in writing this letter was to put Timothy on his guard, and to charge him to use care concerning certain emissaries of a legal system who were moving about among the early Christian churches, seeking to pervert believers from the simplicity that is in Christ. This system was based partly on the law of Moses and partly on Eastern mystical traditions. It developed in after years into what became known down through the centuries as *Gnosticism,* the advocates of which claimed they had a superior knowledge not vouchsafed to other Christians. They sought to gain as many proselytes to their system as they possibly could.

Paul stressed the importance of faith in Christ, which involves salvation by grace alone and not by works of righteousness which we have done, or by any fancied merit of our own. He shows that we are saved by grace alone, and when we have trusted in the Lord Jesus Christ and are justified by faith, that faith results in the love of God being shed abroad in our hearts. With this comes ready obedience, but not as a matter of legality. It is easy to do the things which please God when we love Him supremely. The heart readily seeks to please those whom we love, and so the apostle says, "Now the end of the commandment [the charge he was giving to Timothy] is charity." Our old English word *charity* really means "love." "[Love] out of a pure heart, and of a good conscience, and [the manifestation] of faith unfeigned."

When one's conscience is aroused and is seized with the terror of the law, when he realizes that he is lost, then he can never find real rest or peace until he finds it in the finished work of the Lord Jesus Christ. When he sees that all his sins have been put away by that work, then his conscience is purged, and he is at peace with God. With this is linked the communication of a new life. The believer in Christ is born again, and being born of God, he has a new nature that delights in holiness, purity, and goodness. He is actually a partaker of the divine nature. Therefore he loves God. He loves his fellow Christians. He loves lost men who are still in darkness and living according to the course of this world. This is why genuine Christians are willing to sacrifice in order that they may win others to Christ.

It is this that Paul emphasizes in writing to the younger preacher, Timothy. He stresses the need of preaching the Word, the importance of this gospel of Christ which is the sole remedy for sin. Some had swerved from this and had turned aside unto vain jangling because false teachers had gotten into the church, and some were not strong enough to resist them and so were carried away by their specious theories. They had swerved from the simplicity that is in Christ. It is ever the object of the Devil to obscure the truth and get Christians occupied with something that will hide the glorious face of the Lord Jesus Christ and becloud the truth regarding His finished work.

Such evil teachers were active at Ephesus where Timothy was laboring: "Desiring to be teachers of the law; understanding neither what they say, nor whereof they affirm." These self-appointed teachers had no knowledge of that which they professed to proclaim. They displayed their own ignorance as they sought to add law to grace. This very fact proved that they did not know what they were talking about, because law and grace will no more mix than will water and oil. They are two altogether different principles. The law says, "Be good, and I will bless you"; grace says, "I have blessed you, now be good." They are opposites. The law says, *"Do* this, and thou shalt live"; grace says, *"Believe* this, and thou shalt live." Law demands; grace freely bestows.

Paul says that we know the law is good. We do not ignore the importance of law; we do not set aside the authority of the Ten Commandments. Preachers of grace are often asked if the Ten Commandments were ever abrogated. No, the law remains with all its stern demands. But the believer has died to the law in the Person of Christ, who is the end of the law to every one that believes. But to the unsaved the law speaks as loudly as ever: "We know that the law is good, if a man use it lawfully; knowing this, that the law is not made for a righteous man, but for the lawless and disobedient, for the ungodly and for sinners, for unholy and profane." By the term *righteous* here we are to understand those who have been made righteous in Christ. The law is for the lawless and disobedient. It is not designed to show spiritually-minded believers how to behave.

If you are a Christian you do not refrain from taking the name of God in vain because you learn it is contrary to law. You love your heavenly Father, and because you love Him you would not think of using His name carelessly. Every Christian knows the sense of shock, of displeasure, that comes whenever he hears the name of God the Father or of the Lord Jesus Christ used profanely. Why is it that it stirs us when many of us were not concerned about such language as this before we were saved? It is because we have now a new nature, a new love for the Lord Jesus Christ and for God who, in His mercy, has brought us to know Himself. And so, I repeat, it is not the law which teaches us how to behave. If we refrain from stealing it is not because the law says "Thou shalt not steal," but because we have no desire to steal, even if we were ever addicted to such wickedness as this before we were saved. Now our desire is to be a blessing to others and not to wrong them in any way. Thus we see that the law is not for righteous men and women.

What then is the standard of the righteous? It is Christ Himself. The Word of God reveals Him as our example, and we seek to walk as He walked. The consistent believer seeks to be like Him, to love as He loves, and to behave as He would behave. The righteousness of which the apostle speaks is a righteousness that springs from a renewed mind. We delight to honor the One who redeemed us.

The law still speaks to the ungodly. It convicts the sinner of his lawlessness. In 1 John 3:4 we read, "Whosoever committeth sin transgresseth also the law: for sin is the transgression of the law." But this is not exactly what John meant, as every careful Greek scholar knows. It might be better translated, "sin is lawlessness." Sin is self-will. It defies the law of God, which insists on righteousness. "Knowing this, that the law is not made for a righteous man, but for the lawless and disobedient, for the ungodly and for sinners, for unholy and profane, for murderers of fathers and murderers of mothers, for manslayers." Is not that rather strange? It is not murderers in general who are mentioned, but "murderers of fathers and murderers of mothers," as though to put it in the very strongest sense. The law says, "Thou shalt not kill." That forbids all murder.

Let me say this, dear young people, you do not have to stab your mother with a knife or a dagger, or strike your father with a club in order to kill them. You can kill them by your willfulness. Many a dear mother has gone down to an early grave heartbroken because of the evil behavior of a loved son or daughter, and many a father has sunk under the awful blow of a son or daughter who turned away from the path of righteousness. We need to remember that murder does not necessarily mean driving a knife into the heart or mixing a cup of poison, but it may consist of anything that breaks a dear one's health and results in early death. And so the law is given for the lawless, those who would destroy others.

Note the awful list of sinners mentioned in verse 10: "For whoremongers, for them that defile themselves with mankind, for menstealers, for liars, for perjured persons, and if there be any other thing that is contrary to sound doctrine." I have heard people say, "Why does the Bible have those nasty words in it? I do not like to read them, and I do not like to hear them read from the pulpit." It is not the words that are so bad; it is the vile sins that they represent. The Holy Spirit always uses the right words to describe these shameful sins in order that men might realize their wickedness and corruption when they indulge in such sins as these.

If I dared to believe all that I am told by Christian high school teachers and college professors, I would have to believe that many of the youth of our land today are becoming almost as corrupt as the people before the flood, and conditions are as vile as those in Sodom and Gomorrah when those cities were destroyed with fire from heaven. From what these teachers tell us, many young people of high school and college age, as well as older people, are given to the very sins depicted here. But to everyone comes that stern command, "Thou shalt not commit adultery," and that covers every kind of sexual evil. If people would only listen to the voice of the law we would never have such terrible crimes against children and others which have become so prevalent in this and other enlightened lands. God's law is defied, and so sin flaunts itself openly and men glory in their shame.

The law is given for liars. "Thou shalt not bear false witness against thy neighbour." Men are in the habit of distinguishing between different types of lies. Some lies are called "white lies," and some are called "black lies." But my Bible tells me, "All liars, shall have their part in the lake which burneth with fire and brimstone" (Rev. 21:8). It does not make any distinction between white, black, and gray lies. So the commandment comes to every untruthful person, condemning falsehood of every description.

"And if there be any other thing that is contrary to sound doctrine." In other words, the law was given to convict men of every sort of sinfulness and wickedness. All such are exposed to the righteous judgment of God. "For as many as are of the works of the law are under the curse: for it is written, Cursed is every one that continueth not in all things which are written in the book of the law to do them" (Gal. 3:10). The only way one can ever escape that curse is by personal faith in the Lord Jesus Christ. He died to redeem us from the curse of the law; He was made a curse for us: "Christ hath redeemed us from the curse of the law, being made a curse for us: for it is written, Cursed is every one that hangeth on a tree" (Gal. 3:13).

"If there be any other thing that is contrary to sound doctrine." Notice how frequently Paul uses this word *sound.* Of course I realize he was writing by inspiration; nevertheless, it appealed to his own heart. *Sound* means "healthy," and when the apostle speaks of *sound* doctrine, he means doctrines that are conducive to spiritual health.

If we will turn to some of the other passages in these Pastoral Epistles where he uses this word, it will help us to get the force of it: "If any man teach otherwise, and consent not to wholesome [that is, *sound*] words, even the words of our Lord Jesus Christ, and to the doctrine which is according to godliness" (1 Tim. 6:3). "Hold fast the form of *sound* words, which thou hast heard of me, in faith and love which is in Christ Jesus" (2 Tim. 1:13). "For the time will come when they will not endure *sound* doctrine; but after their own lusts shall they heap to themselves teachers, having itching ears" (2 Tim. 4:3). "Holding fast the faithful word as he hath been taught, that he may be able by *sound* doctrine both to exhort and to convince the gainsayers" (Titus 1:9). "But speak thou the things which become *sound* doctrine: that the aged men be sober, grave, temperate, *sound* in faith, in charity, in patience" (Titus 2:1–2).

Through all these Pastoral Epistles, Paul emphasizes the importance of teaching the spiritually healthful doctrine. The proclamation of the truth of God's Word is conducive to health spiritually. False teaching leads to death and decay. Where the teaching in the classroom and from the pulpit is sound, it has an effect for good, and tends to build up believers in holiness of life and Christlikeness in character. Where it is otherwise, it has the very opposite effect.

Paul concludes this section with the words, "According to the glorious gospel of the blessed God, which was committed to my trust." Now in order to get the connection we should notice that all that is included from the first word of verse 6 to the last word in verse 10 came in parenthetically. Go back to verse 5, "Now the end of the commandment is charity out of a pure heart, and of a good conscience, and of faith unfeigned"; now verse 11: "According to the glorious gospel of the blessed God, which was committed to my trust." The glorious gospel is really the gospel of the glory. It is an expression peculiar to the apostle Paul. In 2 Corinthians 4:4 he says, "In whom the god of this world hath blinded the minds of them which believe not, lest the light of the glorious gospel of Christ, who is the image of God, should shine unto them."

Paul spoke of the gospel as the gospel of the glory because it tells of a glorified Christ, a Christ who once bore our sins when He hung as a bleeding Victim on Calvary that we might become the righteousness of God in Him. He is now the glorified Man seated on the right hand of God in heaven, and Paul was eager to proclaim the message about that Man in the glory, so he calls his message the gospel of the glory. This is the message that has been passed on to us. A glorified Christ at the Father's right hand tells us that the sin question is settled, and now God can save in righteousness all who come to Him and believe in His Son.

CHAPTER 3

The Chief of Sinners Saved

1 Timothy 1:12–17

> And I thank Christ Jesus our Lord, who hath enabled me, for that he counted me faithful, putting me into the ministry; who was before a blasphemer, and a persecutor, and injurious: but I obtained mercy, because I did it ignorantly in unbelief. And the grace of our Lord was exceeding abundant with faith and love which is in Christ Jesus. This is a faithful saying, and worthy of all acceptation, that Christ Jesus came into the world to save sinners; of whom I am chief. Howbeit for this cause I obtained mercy, that in me first Jesus Christ might show forth all longsuffering, for a pattern to them which should hereafter believe on him to life everlasting. Now unto the King eternal, immortal, invisible, the only wise God, be honour and glory for ever and ever. Amen. (vv. 12–17)

There is tremendous power in Christian testimony. All who are saved are not called to be preachers; all do not have the gift of teaching. But all who have trusted in the Lord Jesus Christ ought to have something to say about the great change that comes into the life when Christ is received as Savior and owned as Lord. The apostle Peter tells us we ought to "be ready always to give an answer to every man that asketh you a reason of the hope that is in you with meekness and fear" (1 Peter 3:15). We may not know very much about theology. We may not be very familiar with the deeper Christian doctrines. But if we have definitely trusted Christ, we ought to be able to say with the one-time blind man of John 9, "One thing I know, that, whereas I was blind, now I see" (v. 25). We were blind before we saw the Savior, but when He revealed Himself to us His glory shone through those darkened lids of the eyes of our souls, opened them, and lighted them forever.

I know there are some people who are inclined to discount Christian testimonies. They do not seem to enjoy meetings in which people come together to tell what the Lord has done for them. But it seems to me that the way the Lord uses testimonies in the New Testament ought to be a rebuke to them. Take, for instance, this case of Saul who became the apostle Paul, the writer of this letter to Timothy.

We have the story of his conversion at least six times in the New Testament. In Acts 9 we have the historical account of his conversion. In Acts 22 we find him telling about it to his Jewish brethren on the steps of the fortress by the temple in Jerusalem. In Acts 26 we find him relating his experience again before the Roman governor Festus, King Agrippa, and his consort, Bernice. Then in the epistle to the Galatians, chapters 1 and 2, Paul goes over the wondrous story once more, and he tells how he, the one-time enemy of the cross of Christ, reached the place where God revealed His Son in him. In Philippians 3 we have his testimony repeated. He tells us of his religion before he saw the Lord; and how afterward, because of that wondrous vision of Christ in glory, he was able to say: "But what things were gain to me, those I counted loss for Christ. Yea doubtless, and I count all things but loss for the excellency of the knowledge of Christ Jesus my Lord: for whom I have suffered the loss of all things, and do count them but dung, that I may win Christ" (Phil. 3:7–8). Then here in the first epistle to Timothy, in this opening chapter, he says, "And I thank Christ Jesus our Lord, who hath enabled me, for that he counted me faithful, putting me into the ministry; who was before a blasphemer, and a persecutor, and injurious: but I obtained mercy, because I did it ignorantly in unbelief."

There are many people who profess to be Christians who do not have any conversion story to tell. Of course I recognize the fact that some came to Christ early in life as mere children, and they have but a hazy recollection, if any remembrance at all, of what took place at the time. We are not to discount their conversions because they cannot give a clear account of them. The Lord Jesus said to adults, "Except ye be converted, and become as little children, ye shall not enter into the kingdom of heaven" (Matt. 18:3). Children are ideal subjects of the kingdom. It is wonderful to win the children to Christ before they come to know anything of the wickedness and corruption of this world. I know some people sneer at child conversion, but it is a great thing to save the children.

An evangelist had spoken on several occasions in a particular church. On one occasion he met some friends after the meeting, and one asked, "Any results from your message tonight?" The evangelist said, "Yes, three and one-half converts." The friend said, "You mean there were three adults and one child." "No," replied the evangelist, "there were three children and one adult." The three children have their whole lives before them, but the adult has lived half his life and has only a fraction left. That is the reason the evangelist said "three and one-half converts." That ought to be a word of encouragement to all Sunday school teachers and young people's workers to sow the seed in the hearts of boys and girls. Remember, it is the incorruptible seed, and you can count on it to spring forth into life.

If people have passed through the years of childhood and come up to youth or maturity without accepting Christ, and then at last are convicted by the Spirit of God of sin, righteousness, and judgment, and they turn to the Lord and trust Him as Savior, they ought to have a very definite story of conversion to tell. They should certainly know this: that they were lost sinners. They were helpless. They were unable to save themselves. Then they heard the voice of Jesus bidding them come to Him, and they came in all their sin and guilt. They trusted Him, and He saved them. They ought to know the reality of the new birth.

The apostle said, "I thank Christ Jesus our Lord, who hath enabled me." Stop there for a moment. "Enabled me!" How many people there are, when you speak to them of the importance of coming to Christ, who will say, "Yes, I would like to become a Christian, but I am afraid I would not be strong enough to live the Christian life. I do not want to make a profession and break down, and thus bring dishonor on the name of the Lord." If it depended upon us, we certainly would break down. But when we once trust Christ as our Savior and are born of God, the Holy Spirit comes to dwell within us, to be the power of the new life; it is He who enables us to live for God and serve Him as we seek to make His gospel known to others. It was this over which Paul rejoiced.

"I thank Christ Jesus our Lord, who hath enabled me, for that he counted me faithful, putting me into the ministry." Do not misunderstand the expression "counted me faithful." Saul of Tarsus had been unfaithful. The word for "faithful" is the same as "believing." "He counted me to be a believer." And whenever anyone believes in the Lord Jesus Christ, God saves him. And He saves us in order that we may serve Him. Paul says, "He counted me *to be a believer,* putting me into the ministry." That is the only way one ever becomes a true minister of Christ. He must be put into the ministry by the Lord Himself.

There are some men who have become ministers simply by solicitation or advice of friends or relatives. Others have "entered the ministry," as it is called, because of worldly ambition. They think of it as one of the learned professions where there is an opportunity to give one's self to the study of social problems, religious theories, and other interesting questions. Again, others are moved by a real compassion for the souls of men, and they endeavor to qualify as pastors and leaders in Christian work in order to carry out humanitarian plans for the alleviation of the miseries of underprivileged people. Some of these motives are good and some are not. But it is not in any of these ways that God makes ministers. He takes men up in mercy, saves them by His grace, and puts into their hearts a burning desire to make Christ known to the world. That is what He did for Saul of Tarsus. When God makes a man a minister, His word is as a fire in his soul, and he can say, "Woe is me if I preach not the gospel."

"Who was before a blasphemer, and a persecutor, and injurious: but I obtained mercy, because I did it ignorantly in unbelief." Paul never could forgive himself for this in after years. He says in one place, "For I am the least of the apostles, that am not meet to be called an apostle, because I persecuted the church of God" (1 Cor. 15:9). And again, we read in Acts 22:20, "And when the blood of thy martyr Stephen was shed, I also was standing by, and consenting unto his death, and kept the raiment of them that slew him." Paul looked back with horror upon those years. He was intensely sincere at the time. A man can be very sincere in wrong things. "I verily thought with myself, that I ought to do many things contrary to the name of Jesus of Nazareth. Which thing I also did in Jerusalem: and many of the saints did I shut up in prison, having received authority from the chief priests; and when they were put to death, I gave my voice against them" (Acts 26:9–10). God in grace saved him, and all that was put away. But Paul never forgave himself to the day of his death for the part he had taken in persecuting the church of God. He says, "I obtained mercy, because I did it ignorantly in unbelief." The poet was right when he wrote:

> There's a wideness in God's mercy,
> Like the wideness of the sea;
> There's a kindness in His justice,
> Which is more than liberty.
>
> For the love of God is broader
> Than the measure of man's mind;

And the heart of the Eternal
Is most wonderfully kind.

Saul of Tarsus was persecuting the church of God. But even then the heart of God was going out toward him until the time when His grace should be revealed to him, and Saul the persecutor should be changed into Paul the Ambassador of Christ. God had mercy on him because he acted in ignorance. He was sure that Christianity was all wrong. He did not understand until the day when he caught sight of the risen Christ in glory. "And the grace of our Lord was exceeding abundant with faith and love which is in Christ Jesus." Immediately after his conversion he began preaching Christ. "And straightway he preached Christ in the synagogues, that he is the Son of God. But all that heard him were amazed, and said; Is not this he that destroyed them which called on this name in Jerusalem, and came hither for that intent, that he might bring them bound unto the chief priests?" (Acts 9:20–21).

It was grace that so mightily changed Saul: grace broke him down on the Damascus road; grace brought Ananias to him to give him a special message, showing how gladly the church of God would receive him when he put his trust in the Savior; grace empowered him to go forth and preach the gospel. The man who goes forth to preach Christ must go in faith and love—faith in the One who lives to save, love for the souls of lost men. There are many professional ministers today, but a merely professional preacher is an abomination in the sight of God. The servants of God must be motivated by the love of Christ. That was what characterized Paul.

Now we get that wonderful declaration that has been repeated so often by gospel preachers: "This is a faithful saying, and worthy of all acceptation, that Christ Jesus came into the world to save sinners; of whom I am chief." Many have the idea that Christ came to save good people, but He tells us, "I am not come to call the righteous, but sinners to repentance" (Matt. 9:13). Listen to me, if you can prove that you are not a sinner, then I can prove from this Word that Jesus did not come to save you. "They that be whole need not a physician, but they that are sick" (Matt. 9:12). He is the Great Physician, healing sin-sick souls. If you have never come to Him, will you not come today and prove the reality of His saving power? Do not fear that you are too great a sinner. Read the words again: "This is a faithful saying, and worthy of all acceptation, that Christ Jesus came into the world to save sinners; of whom I am chief." The chief of sinners has been saved already, so you can only trail along behind. He who described himself as the chief is now in the glory. Therefore you need not fear lest you are too bad for Christ.

Listen to the apostle's confession, "Howbeit for this cause I obtained mercy, that in me first Jesus Christ might show forth all longsuffering, for a pattern to them which should hereafter believe on him to life everlasting." "I obtained mercy." We do not receive salvation because we deserve it, "but according to his mercy he saved us, by the washing of regeneration, and renewing of the Holy Ghost" (Titus 3:5). Paul says, "That in me first Jesus Christ might show forth all longsuffering, for a pattern to them which should hereafter believe on him to life everlasting." I get two things from that last clause: Paul tells us that the Lord saved him as a pattern. He became a pattern to all future believers—he, the chief sinner, was saved by divine grace. Then I think Paul had this also in mind: he was saved by a revelation of Christ from heaven. Someday his own people Israel are going to have a wonderful revelation of Christ from heaven, and then they, as a nation, will turn to Him. So I believe Paul had Israel in mind when he said that he was a pattern "to them which should hereafter believe on him to life everlasting."

He closes this section with a wonderful doxology. His heart is filled with worship and praise, and he bursts forth in these words, "Now unto the King eternal, immortal [incorruptible], invisible [Deity is invisible to the human eye], the only wise God, be honour and glory for ever and ever. Amen." This is the grateful expression of worship that rises from the heart of the saved sinner. It tells of a soul exulting in the matchless wonder of redeeming love.

CHAPTER 4

Maintaining a Good Conscience

1 Timothy 1:18–20

> This charge I commit unto thee, son Timothy, according to the prophecies which went before on thee, that thou by them mightest war a good warfare; holding faith, and a good conscience; which some having put away concerning faith have made shipwreck: of whom is Hymenaeus and Alexander; whom I have delivered unto Satan, that they may learn not to blaspheme. (vv. 18–20)

We come now to consider the very solemn charge which the apostle Paul gave to his son in the faith. We have already seen that Timothy had been left to help the church at Ephesus. There were special responsibilities resting upon him there, and it was important that he should be careful as to his own walk and testimony in order that he might be an example to others. So Paul says, "This charge I commit unto thee, son Timothy, according to the prophecies which went before on thee, that thou by them mightest war a good warfare."

The Christian life is a conflict, particularly the life of a Christian minister. God desires all His servants to be good soldiers of the Lord Jesus Christ.

Timothy was therefore called to war a good warfare. It is very evident that at the time he was recommended to the work of the Lord by the brethren at Lystra and Iconium that a prayer meeting was held, and as the elder brethren laid hands upon him and commended him to the work of the gospel, in some special way the Lord gave him a gift which before he did not have. We get some intimation of that from Paul's words, "According to the prophecies which went before on thee, that thou by them mightest war a good warfare," and from 4:14 of this letter, "Neglect not the gift that is in thee, which was given thee by prophecy, with the laying on of the hands of the presbytery."

Paul stresses or seeks to impress upon this younger preacher the importance of "holding faith and a good conscience." Notice how these two things go together. It is impossible to hold the faith if one is not careful to maintain a good conscience before God. Here I understand *faith* to mean not merely confidence in God but also the truth of God, the faith once for all delivered unto the saints. Every little while we hear of someone who, in days gone by, was apparently a preacher of the Word giving up the faith that he once proclaimed. Men, who in early days preached the Deity of the Lord Jesus Christ, His atoning, sacrificial death and physical resurrection, no longer proclaim salvation through His blood or the need of the new birth. They have turned from the truth and accepted what some call the "new liberal theological attitude." They have become reprobate concerning the faith.

And people wonder why it is that such men have apostatized from the truth of God which at one time they professed to love. If we were able to look into the lives of these men, we would find that somewhere along the line they failed to respond to the call of God and they put away a good conscience. Thus they lost the ability to properly appraise doctrinal principles, and eventually they found it a relief to give up the truth they once proclaimed. Men do not fall suddenly into grave error. Such failure is the result of permitting the conscience to become denied so that it no longer registers as it once did.

We may spend a little time profitably in looking at a number of Scripture verses in connection with conscience. What is conscience? The word thus translated is really a compound and literally means "co-perception." It is that within us which enables us to distinguish between right and wrong. You remember the little girl who was asked, "Do you know what conscience is?" She replied, "Oh, yes, it is something in me that always tells me when my little brother is doing wrong." That is the way a lot of people look at conscience—something indefinable within them by which they judge other people. Conscience is that which should tell us when we are right and wrong. It is "knowing with oneself." Conscience was acquired by the fall in Eden. There was no need of a monitor to warn unfallen Adam about evil, or to tell him the difference between right and wrong, between sin and righteousness, for he knew only that which was good until he partook of the forbidden fruit. Then he knew good and evil.

Conscience needs to be instructed. When the apostle Paul was making his defense in Jerusalem, he said, "Men and brethren, I have lived in all good conscience before God until this day" (Acts 23:1). When he said that, he was reviewing his whole life before he was converted as well as afterward. Even before he knew Christ he sought to keep a good conscience. In other words, when he persecuted the Christians, he did it with a good conscience; when he tried to destroy the infant church, he acted conscientiously. But his conscience was not properly instructed. He thought it was the right thing to do because he believed that Christianity was an evil system. He believed that Christians were enemies of God and that he was acting in accordance with Scripture which commanded that false prophets be destroyed. He told Agrippa in Acts 26:9–10, "I verily thought with myself, that I ought to do many things contrary to the name of Jesus of Nazareth. Which thing I also did in Jerusalem: and many of the saints did I shut up in prison, having received authority from the chief priests; and when they were put to death, I gave my voice against them." So it is not enough for one to say he lives according to his conscience.

On the other hand, we should not go against conscience, for when we do that the conscience becomes defiled. Conscience needs to be instructed by the Word of God. In Romans 2:14–15 we find that thought carried out. We have seen that conscience is that which bears witness to what is believed to be right and wrong: "For when the Gentiles, which have not the law, do by nature the things contained in the law, these, having not the law, are a law unto themselves: which show the work of the law written in their hearts, their conscience also bearing witness, and their thoughts the mean while accusing or else excusing one another." "Their conscience also bearing witness"—that is true of even the most wicked people, for their own consciences warn them when they are about to do something which they know to be wrong, and conscience accuses or excuses them, according to the measure of light they have.

In Titus 1:15–16 we read of a defiled conscience: "Unto the pure all things are pure: but unto them that are defiled and unbelieving is nothing pure; but even their mind and conscience is defiled. They profess that they know God; but in works they deny him, being abominable, and disobedient, and unto every good work reprobate." These verses tell us of the condition of unconverted people who have turned away from that which they knew to be right morally. They knew how they ought to live, but they did the opposite. Consequently, the conscience became defiled, and a defiled conscience is no longer a safe guide.

In Hebrews 10:22 we read, "Let us [the apostle is speaking to Christians] draw near with a true heart in full assurance of faith, having our hearts sprinkled from an evil conscience, and our bodies washed with pure water." An evil conscience is the result of persistence in sin. If men continue to defile themselves, the time will come when the conscience becomes thoroughly evil, and sin is no longer dreaded. When we come to Christ our hearts are sprinkled from an evil conscience. If men do not come to Him but insist on sinning against the light, refusing to heed the invitation which God has extended to all men to turn to Him in repentance and be saved, then eventually the conscience ceases to be active. It becomes seared. "Now the Spirit speaketh expressly, that in the latter times some shall depart from the faith, giving heed to seducing spirits, and doctrines of devils; speaking lies in hypocrisy; having their consciences seared with a hot iron" (1 Tim. 4:1–2).

This is most solemn. Sin hardens. The conscience becomes like flesh that has been seared with a hot iron. It no longer responds. It can no longer be depended upon. In this state men may commit the most wicked and abominable things, and apparently there is not the least exercise of conscience. It is because they have gone so far in disobeying that which they knew to be right that they no longer have any concern whatsoever. They are given up to a seared conscience and a reprobate mind, and with that comes utter hardness of heart. But if men are willing to turn to God, if they realize they have an evil conscience and long for a pure and a cleansed conscience, they may obtain it through the work of the cross.

In Hebrews 9:9–10 the apostle is speaking of the various ordinances of the Levitical economy, "Which was a figure for the time then present, in which were offered both gifts and sacrifices, that could not make him that did the service perfect, as pertaining to the conscience; which stood only in meats and drinks, and divers washings, and carnal ordinances, imposed on them until the time of reformation." That is, the sacrifices offered on Jewish altars could not give a man a perfect conscience. They could not cleanse his defiled conscience, nor free him of an evil conscience. But the Lord Jesus Christ has offered Himself as an all-sufficient sacrifice for sin.

We read in verses 13–14 of the same chapter of Hebrews, "For if the blood of bulls and of goats, and the ashes of an heifer sprinkling the unclean, sanctifieth to the purifying of the flesh: how much more shall the blood of Christ, who through the eternal Spirit offered himself without spot to God, purge your conscience from dead works to serve the living God?" Knowing that the sin question has been settled to God's satisfaction the troubled soul can afford to rest in the knowledge of what Christ has done, and so the conscience no longer accuses but is purified by faith, because the blood of Christ, God's Son, cleanses from every sin all those who come out from the darkness of nature into the light of God's presence, in which they walk ever afterward. Now as believers we are responsible to walk before God with a good conscience.

Let us turn back to 1 Timothy, and notice a verse which we have considered already in these addresses: "Now the end of the commandment is charity out of a pure heart, and of a good conscience, and of faith unfeigned" (1:5). Then in this same chapter, the verse which we read at the beginning of our present study: "This charge I commit unto thee, son Timothy, according to the prophecies which went before on thee, that thou by them mightest war a good warfare; holding faith, and a good conscience; which some having put away concerning faith have made shipwreck." Both the apostles Paul and Peter stress the importance of maintaining a good and pure conscience. In 1 Peter 3:16 we read, "Having a good conscience; that, whereas they speak evil of you, as of evildoers, they may be ashamed that falsely accuse your good conversation in Christ."

Let me just add this word while on the subject of conscience. You and I are responsible to be careful not to offend needlessly the conscience of a weaker brother. Some people are very legal. They are exercised about matters with which stronger Christians are not concerned. And so those who perhaps fancy they are stronger are warned to be careful in this matter of conscience. I am my brother's keeper. I am not to allow myself to indulge in anything that will offend or stumble one who is weak. This is very important, as we may bring grievous injury upon the soul of another if we insist on our liberty in that which to him may seem a very grave offense.

"Holding faith, and a good conscience; which some having put away concerning faith have made shipwreck." There were those who had turned from the great fundamental principles of Christianity and were living in ways displeasing to God. They had put away a good conscience. They knew what God's Word required of them but went against their own consciences, and little by little they got to the place where they were no longer very much exercised. The conscience is like a rubber band. You pull it, and it snaps back. You pull it again, and it snaps back. But if you keep on pulling it, by-and-by it loses its elasticity and, finally, does not snap back at all. It is very dangerous to trifle with conscience, for if we act contrary to this inward monitor, we find the reaction becomes less and less, until eventually there is no reaction at all. Then we are likely to make shipwreck of the faith.

It is easy to lose the truth of God if we do not live in obedience to the Word. We do not hold the truth simply in the mind. We learn it through the heart and the conscience, and we hold it by keeping a conscience that is void of offense.

Paul here mentions two men who had turned from the truth and were propagating blasphemous error. They had put away a good conscience and so had turned from the truth of God. Paul says that he delivered them unto Satan that they might learn not to blaspheme. They were excommunicated from Christian fellowship and put back into the world that they might learn not to play fast-and-loose with that which God had revealed. John tells us that we—that is, Christians—are of God, and the whole world lies in the wicked one. We are warned, "Love not the world, neither the things that are in the world" (1 John 2:15). When we profess Christ we step out from the world and come into Christian fellowship. We are separated to the Lord, and we should maintain that separation constantly. These two men had professed to know and love Christ, but they had departed from the truth. The apostle commanded that they be put outside the fellowship of the church of God. In other words, thrown back into the world which at one time they professed to have forsaken. They were delivered unto Satan "that they may learn not to blaspheme." Discipline should always be with a view to restoration. In 1 Corinthians 5:5 we read, "To deliver such an one unto Satan for the destruction of the flesh, that the spirit may be saved in the day of the Lord Jesus."

So the important lesson for us all is the necessity of maintaining a good conscience before God. We should not become careless as to our behavior in regard to that which pleases the blessed One who loved us enough to shed His precious blood to redeem us from the bondage of our sins.

CHAPTER 5

UNLIMITED REDEMPTION

1 Timothy 2:1–7

> I exhort therefore, that, first of all, supplications, prayers, intercessions, and giving of thanks, be made for all men; for kings, and for all that are in authority; that we may lead a quiet and peaceable life in all godliness and honesty. For this is good and acceptable in the sight of God our Saviour; who will have all men to be saved, and to come unto the knowledge of the truth. For there is one God, and one mediator between God and men, the man Christ Jesus; who gave himself a ransom for all, to be testified in due time. Whereunto I am ordained a preacher, and an apostle, (I speak the truth in Christ, and lie not;) a teacher of the Gentiles in faith and verity. (vv. 1–7)

In these verses we have an earnest exhortation and a very marvelous declaration, and the two are most intimately linked together. The exhortation has to do with our responsibility in respect to prayer. We read in the first verse, "I exhort therefore, that, first of all, supplications, prayers, intercessions, and giving of thanks, be made for all men." One of the first great responsibilities resting upon the people of God is supplication and prayer.

Four things are brought before us here. The word *prayer* suggests any kind of approach to God as we draw near to Him to present those things that are on our hearts. The word *supplication* goes somewhat deeper, and has to do with matters about which we are greatly exercised and which cause intense concern. The word *intercession* suggests prayer on behalf of others. Our blessed Lord "ever liveth to make intercession for [us]" (Heb. 7:25). And now while we are here on earth it is our privilege to intercede on behalf of fellow saints, on behalf of Israel, on behalf of the nations generally, on behalf of unsaved people that they might be brought to know the Lord, and on behalf of rulers that they might be guided aright.

With prayers, supplications, and intercessions we always should link thanksgiving. In Philippians 4:6 the apostle says, "Be careful for nothing; but in every thing by prayer and supplication with thanksgiving let your requests be made known unto God." When we come to God in prayer to supplicate for needed blessings or to intercede on behalf of others, we should not be ungrateful as we think of His dealings with us in the past. You will remember that in 2 Timothy 3:2 unthankfulness is connected with unholiness. Thankfulness and gratitude to God, and holiness of heart and life are linked intimately together.

Notice the scope of intercession in the last part of the first verse and in verse 2. We are to pray for *all men.* We can do that only in a general way. We do not know what the will of God is as to the lives of all men, but we learn from the following declaration that it is God's desire that all men should be saved. So we can pray in fellowship with God that the Holy Spirit may bring men under conviction of sin, to confess their lost condition, and to see their need of Christ. We are not to confine our prayer to just a few of our own little circle, but our hearts are to go out to all men. We are to pray in a special sense for those who have been given responsibility as rulers, in all nations. God Himself it is who has divided us into nations, and it is God who puts one man up and another down. It is He who gives authority to different men, and they are responsible—those who are placed in positions of leadership—to act in accordance with the Lord's will. They do not always do it. In fact, very infrequently perhaps are they concerned about doing the will of God. But, as Christians, we may help them in this by prayer.

We are to pray "for kings, and for all that are in authority." When we come together in a public service, we usually pray for those who are in authority. But are we as much concerned about remembering them before God when we kneel alone in His presence? I am quite sure of this: if we prayed more for those at the head of the country and in other positions of responsibility, we would feel less ready to criticize them. We would be more disposed to recognize the heavy burdens resting upon them and to understand how easy it is to make mistakes in times of crises. Our rulers need divine wisdom that they might govern well in subjection to Him who is earth's rightful King. As we pray earnestly for them, we are furthering our own best interests. Because as the affairs of nations are ordered according to the will of God, His people find living conditions more comfortable and more enjoyable. So we are told to pray "for all that are in authority; that we may lead a quiet and peaceable life in all godliness and honesty."

Christians are to be examples to others of subjection to the government. When difficulties arise and differences come up that divide people and set one group against another, we should be characterized by quiet, restful confidence in God as we refer these things to Him in prayer. God told Israel, when they were scattered among the nations of the earth, to pray for the peace of the different lands in which they dwelt. This is a responsibility that rests upon us as believers today.

"For this is good and acceptable in the sight of God our Saviour." The apostle uses this beautiful term—"God our Saviour"—a number of times in this epistle. How precious it is to think of God in that connection! In our unsaved state we knew Him as God the Judge, but now since we have come to know Him as revealed in Christ, He has become God our Savior.

We get a very definite reason why we should pray for all men: God our Savior wills, that is, He desires to have, "all men to be saved, and to come unto the knowledge of the truth." I hope we believe that. I find that some of my brethren do not seem to believe it. They speak as though there are some men whom God has brought into existence for whom there is no possibility of salvation because they are not among the elect. I find no such teaching as this in Scripture. We read in that wonderful passage—the miniature Bible, as Luther calls it—"For God so loved the world, that he gave his only begotten Son, that whosoever believeth in him should not perish, but have everlasting life" (John 3:16). Thank God, we can go to men everywhere and tell them,

> There is plentiful redemption
> In the blood that has been shed.

No matter how far they have drifted from God, no matter what their sins may be, they do not have to peer into the book of the divine decrees in order to find out whether or not they are of the chosen or the elect. If they come in all their sin and guilt, confessing their iniquities and trusting in Christ, then they may have the assurance from His Word that they are saved. It has been well said that the "Whosoever *wills* are the elect, and whosoever *won'ts* are the non-elect." All who will may come. Jesus said to those who refused His testimony, "Ye will not come to me, that ye might have life" (John 5:40). It is the desire of God that all men should be saved. He says, "Say unto them, As I live, saith the Lord GOD, I have no pleasure in the death of the wicked; but that the wicked turn from his way and live: turn ye, turn ye from your evil ways; for why will ye die, O house of Israel?" (Ezek. 33:11). This expresses His attitude toward all men everywhere. But their salvation depends upon their coming to the knowledge of the truth—that is, believing the gospel.

Yes, God desires that all men should be saved, and He has made provision whereby all may be saved if they will: "For there is one God, and one mediator between God and men, the man Christ Jesus; who gave himself a ransom for all, to be testified in due time." This is the gospel. It is our responsibility to carry it to the world. There is one God. All other objects that men worship as gods are only idols. They are powerless to save. There is "one mediator between God and men, the man Christ Jesus." He it was who came down from heaven and took humanity into union with His Deity in order to make God known to men, and to give Himself a ransom for all. Now He has gone back to God on behalf of men. He ever lives to intercede for us. Scripture does not know of any other mediator. The blessed Virgin Mary is never referred to in the Bible in this capacity. Nor do we read of saints or angels as mediators. Our Lord Jesus alone stands between us and God, even as His work on the cross is the only ground of our salvation.

He who desires to know God, to be assured of sins forgiven is directed to Jesus by the Holy Spirit, speaking through this Word. "There is none other name under heaven given among men, whereby we must be saved" (Acts 4:12). And, thank God, no other is needed. That name is all-sufficient. He came to earth to give His life a ransom for us. He tells us Himself that, "The Son of man came not to be ministered unto, but to minister, and to give his life a ransom for many" (Matt. 20:28). Some might think the word *many* there indicates that His redemption is not available for all, but the Holy Spirit negates that thought by what we read here in verse 6: "Who gave himself a ransom *for all,* to be testified in due time." While it is true that only those who believe on Him will be actually redeemed, yet He gave Himself an available ransom for all. If ever you are lost eternally, it will not be because God was not ready to save you. If you are shut away from the Home of the Blessed for the ages to come, it will not be because there was not a welcome for you if you had come by way of Calvary's cross. There is no other way, no other salvation than through the redemptive work of the Lord Jesus Christ, and that work avails for you if you will come and put your trust in Him who accomplished it.

This is the message that Paul carried through the world, "Whereunto I am ordained a preacher, and an apostle, (I speak the truth in Christ, and lie not;) a teacher of the Gentiles in faith and verity." Who ordained Paul? Some would say that Ananias ordained him, but who ordained Ananias? From the record he does not seem to have had any special human ordination. But who ordained Paul? The Lord tells us, "I have appeared unto thee for this purpose, to make thee a minister and a witness both of these things which thou hast seen, and of those things in the which I will appear unto thee" (Acts 26:16). So Paul's ordination came when the blessed Lord Jesus appeared to him on the Damascus turnpike, and Paul could have said in the words of the beautiful seventeenth-century poem, which has been rendered into English by Frances Bevan:

> Christ the Son of God hath sent me
> Through the midnight lands:
> Mine the mighty ordination
> Of the pierced hands.

The Lord ordained Paul as preacher and apostle to go to the Gentiles with the gospel of a full redemption whereby all men might be saved. This was the special mission committed to him. And while he never forgot his Jewish brethren as he went from place to place—he usually sought them out first—his great work was to make the gospel known to the Gentile world. And what a world it was! It was a world literally rotten in its vileness and corruption. A world given to the worst kind of paganism and idolatry. A world in which men were enslaved by the Devil and powerless to deliver themselves. It was into such a world as this that the apostle Paul proclaimed the One "who gave himself a ransom for all." And when men believed the message they were saved. They were transformed, and they who had been led by Satan captives of his will became captives in the chains of love, delighting to serve the One who had died to redeem them.

CHAPTER 6

The Consistent Christian Woman

1 Timothy 2:8–15

> I will therefore that men pray every where, lifting up holy hands, without wrath and doubting. In like manner also, that women adorn themselves in modest apparel, with shamefacedness and sobriety; not with broided hair, or gold, or pearls, or costly array; but (which becometh women professing godliness) with good works. Let the woman learn in silence with all subjection. But I suffer not a woman to teach, nor to usurp authority over the man, but to be in silence. For Adam was first formed, then Eve. And Adam was not deceived, but the woman being deceived was in the transgression. Notwithstanding she shall be saved in childbearing, if they continue in faith and charity and holiness with sobriety. (vv. 8–15)

In the first part of this chapter we considered the exhortation to pray for kings, for all who are in authority, and for all men everywhere. We noticed that the exhortation was based on the fact that it is the will of God that all men be saved. All men will not be saved, but that is because they set their desires against God's desire. He desires them to be saved. They desire to fulfill the lusts of the flesh and to live in opposition to the will of God. But if people repent and turn to God, no matter what the record may have been, no matter how sinful and vile, there is forgiveness, abundant grace in the heart of God and sufficient merit in the work of our Lord Jesus Christ whereby all may be saved.

Having dealt with the theme of plenteous redemption, the Apostle goes back to the subject of prayer and stresses the importance of holiness of life if one would pray aright. God has never promised to answer a prayer that comes through unclean lips. True prayer must be backed up by a holy life.

We read, "I will therefore that men pray every where, lifting up holy hands, without wrath and doubting." There are three things to note here. First, prayer, in order to be effectual, must come from those who are seeking to walk in holiness before God. All men are entitled to approach God, but they must be careful that they are living such lives as will commend their prayers to God. If people are living in unholiness and uncleanness, they have no right to pray. They have no title to pray. God has never promised to hear the prayers of people who are not walking righteously before Him. So many people neglect prayer until some great crisis comes. They drift along, toying with their consciences, putting away a good conscience, and allowing themselves to do things which at first conscience condemns and to which afterward it becomes indifferent because of repeated offenses. And then comes the time when they want to pray. They feel the need of prayer. Perhaps some loved one is seriously ill, and they try to pray for his recovery, and then they find that their prayers are hindered because of unjudged sin in the heart. We can pray with confidence only when our prayer is backed up by a godly life. "I will therefore that men pray every where, lifting up holy hands, without wrath and doubting."

Second, we are to pray without indignation or malice, but with love to all mankind. God will not answer a prayer calling down punishment on someone else. If we, in our childish, fretful way, should come to God asking Him to deal in judgment with another whom we feel has offended us, we cannot expect God to hear such a prayer. We are to love our enemies and pray for them that persecute us. We are to "lift up holy hands, without wrath and doubting."

Third, the doubter is like one tossed by the waves of the sea. Our Lord Jesus said, "Therefore I say unto you, What things soever ye desire, when ye pray, believe that ye receive them, and ye shall have them" (Mark 11:24). When we pray in faith we are sure that we pray according to the will of God as He makes that known to us through His holy Word. It is important then that the Christian should back up his prayer with a holy life and implicit confidence in God.

Having said this, the Apostle turns to the subject of our sisters in Christ, and brings before us certain things which Christian women need to remember if they would live consistent lives to the glory of God. First he says, "In like manner also, that women adorn themselves in modest apparel, with shamefacedness and sobriety; not with broided hair, or gold, or pearls, or costly array." *Shamefacedness* is really "shamefastness"—standing fast in modesty, not bold or self-assertive, nor flaunting personal charms in a way that careless, godless women of the world do.

"But (which becometh women professing godliness) with good works." I would rather listen to some fine Christian woman expound these verses than stand up here, a man, and talk to my sisters in Christ regarding them. I would rather that one of their own was giving them this message, but it is incumbent on me as Christ's servant to bring before you just what is in His Word. Remember this, no matter how such Scripture verses as these are spurned by the worldly and backslidden, they are just as truly a part of God's Word as John 3:16.

I remember years ago at a special series of meetings a servant of God was opening up many precious truths in connection with our calling in grace, our place in the body of Christ, our inheritance in Him, and other spiritual themes. One lady who attended the meetings was so stirred that she told how these truths had meant much to her and that she had received great blessing from them. Then in the course of the series of messages the preacher came to a certain passage in 1 Corinthians 14 that had to do with women's behavior in the church of God. As he was reading—it was an open Bible class where people were free to ask questions—this same lady who had testified to having found such blessing through the precious Word spoke up and said, "I do not believe that. I think this is all nonsense. Paul was an old bachelor who hated women, and that is why he writes the way he does. We can't depend upon what he says."

The preacher said, "My dear sister, you have been rejoicing in the truth that nothing 'shall be able to separate us from the love of God, which is in Christ Jesus our Lord' (Rom. 8:39), haven't you?"

"Yes," she said, "I do rejoice in that."

"Well," said the preacher, "I am pained to have to inform you that Paul said that, and Paul was an old bachelor, so you can't depend upon what he says! I understand you have been rejoicing in the truth that there is 'one body of which Christ is the head.'"

"Yes," she said, "I rejoice in that too."

"Well, I am sorry to have to tell you that that is something made known to us by Paul, and Paul was an old bachelor, so you can't depend upon what he says."

He went from one Scripture to another, pointing out the truths which were given to us by Paul, until that dear lady burst into tears and said, "May God forgive me. I see now that I have been trifling with the Word of God."

One part of the Word is as truly inspired as another part. When you come across some things in God's Word that you may think are perhaps questionable, remember that the Holy Spirit who presented Christ as Savior, the Holy Spirit who showed how the way into the Holiest has been opened, is the same Holy Spirit of God who tells our sisters how they ought to behave, and how careful they ought to be to maintain feminine modesty.

Let me read it once again: "In like manner also, that women adorn themselves in modest apparel, with shamefacedness and sobriety," not depending on outward things for their charm or glamour, as it is called today. "Not with broided hair, or gold, or pearls, or costly array; but (which becometh women professing godliness) with good works." Oh, how we all appreciate a woman whose adornment consists of the ornament of a meek and quiet spirit, manifested by patient consideration for others and seeking to do the will of God in grace and humility, so that Christ may be magnified in all her ways! Many of us who were brought up in Christian homes can thank God for examples such as we have seen in our own mothers. Many times as I see how some girls and women of today behave, I thank God my dear mother was not one of these painted, bleached-hair, cigarette-smoking, immodestly dressed women, but a sweet, quiet, godly, Christian woman—a mother who brought her children up in the "nurture and admonition of the Lord."

Women, God has given you a wonderful privilege. It is true, as we have heard it said so often, "The hand that rocks the cradle [though we may not have cradles any longer] is the hand that rules the world." It is given to mothers to set such examples before their children that they can count on God to save them in their early days, and where mothers obey what we have here they can expect God to honor their faithful testimony.

Do not misunderstand and think of this passage as absolutely forbidding women to wear comely ornaments. Compare the passage in 1 Peter 3:3–4, "Whose adorning let it not be that outward adorning of plaiting the hair, and of wearing of gold, or of putting on of apparel; but let it be the hidden man of the heart, in that which is not corruptible, even the ornament of a meek and quiet spirit, which is in the sight of God of great price." Now notice that if we were to understand that the Spirit of God is forbidding women to do up their hair neatly or forbidding them to wear an occasional ornament of gold, then He is also forbidding the putting on of apparel—and the unfortunate thing is that too many women seem inclined to take that latter part literally! But women are not to depend on these things for their judgment. A woman might have her hair put up ever so beautifully; be arrayed in the loveliest, costliest kind of gown; and decorated with the most beautiful ornaments but have a hard, cold, unforgiving, vain, unchristian spirit. And so her outward adornment would count for nothing. The real adornment is that which springs from a heart in subjection to the Holy Spirit of God.

Then as we pass on we come to a Scripture against which some of our sisters rebel: "Let the woman learn in silence with all subjection. But I suffer not a woman to teach, nor to usurp authority over the man, but to be in silence." What is the Apostle insisting on here? We note from other Scripture passages that women are permitted to teach in certain circumstances. But here she is forbidden to teach, or to usurp authority over the man but to be in silence. Here and in 1 Corinthians 14:34–35, Paul is speaking of the regular meeting of the assembly when the whole church comes together to worship God, and at that time the man, we are told in Scripture, is to stand before the people as the representative of the Lord Himself who chooses to speak in that way through His servant. Whereas the woman pictures the church itself in subjection to Christ, receiving her instruction from Him. She is not to take a public place as teacher nor usurp authority over the man. This does not mean that she is not to teach at all. The question of women having Bible classes, teaching boys and girls, conducting women's meetings, or even evangelizing—going out and proclaiming Christ to the general public—is not brought up here.

Let me give an illustration which will perhaps make clear what the Apostle is telling us here. I had a rather unusual experience some years ago. I went to a certain summer Bible conference for the first time. On this occasion I was invited by Dr. Torrey. A lady Bible teacher was present whom I had not met before. I think out of mischief Dr. Torrey seated me at the table with that lady, because he knew how I felt as to women preachers. I had the privilege of eating with this gracious lady twice a day, and we became quite well acquainted. As I was coming out of the tabernacle after my address at eleven o'clock one day I noticed a blackboard sign that read, "At four o'clock Miss So-and-so will give an exposition of the book of Acts." I decided I would go and hear her, which I did. At dinner I was in my place ahead of her. When she came in, she shook her finger at me and said, "You should not have attended my meeting. You were there only to embarrass me."

"Why do you say that?" I asked.

"You do not believe in women preachers," she said. "You believe in taking literally those passages of Paul's."

I asked her, "How do you believe in taking them?"

She replied, "Well, I do not know. They have troubled me during most of my ministry. I do know God has given me a gift to teach His Word, and I feel responsible to do that. But I have never understood what Paul meant when he said, 'I suffer not a woman to teach, nor to usurp authority over the man, but to be in silence.'"

I said, "I do not have any trouble about it. When we gathered on Sunday for the regular service where Dr. Torrey was to preach, if you had gotten up and walked up to him and said, 'Dr. Torrey, I understand that passage. I'll do the preaching this morning.' Then I believe you would have been definitely disobeying this command. But when I saw the sign that at four o'clock this afternoon you were going to give an exposition of the book of Acts, I said to myself, 'If Sister Priscilla is going to expound the book of Acts, I can be like Apollos and can sit at her feet, and I'll be glad to do it.' So I went to hear you, and I enjoyed what you said. I got a great deal of help from your address. You did not usurp any authority over me. I went voluntarily to hear you." Everything seemed clear to her then, and she thanked me for what I put before her.

What the Apostle is saying here is that the woman has her place, and the man has his place. We each have our place in nature, and just as the one cannot change places with the other in nature, so we must not attempt to change places in the order of the church of God here on earth. This has nothing whatsoever to do with our place in the new creation. In the new creation before God there is neither male nor female, but all are one in Christ Jesus. When we get Home all differences will be gone forever, and we will be manifestly one in Christ in that day. But here on earth we have different responsibilities.

What would you think of a home where the wife said to her husband, "From now on I am going to be the wage earner. Husband, you look after the children, wash the dishes, clean the house, and I shall go out and earn the money?" That home would be topsy-turvy. God has ordained that the husband should provide the support for the family, and that the wife should care for the home and bring up the children. There may be times when the husband is unfit for employment, perhaps an illness which prevents his going out and working, and the dear, devoted wife will work and support the family. In that case they have to change places. If the husband has enough strength to do the dishes and clean the house and does not do it, he ought to be ashamed. "Husbands, dwell with them according to knowledge, giving honour unto the wife, as unto the weaker vessel" (1 Peter 3:7). A friend once said to me, "Just what does that mean: 'Giving honour unto the wife, as unto the weaker vessel?'" I said, "It means washing the dishes for her when her head aches." God has put each in his place. Mark, it is not that God is discounting the woman and her capabilities, but she has her sphere and the man has his.

The man is more or less dominated by his head—if he has any head; whereas the woman is likely to be controlled by the heart. I have often heard my wife say, "I don't like that man." I would ask, "Why?" "I don't know," she would say. "I just don't like him." "Well, why don't you like him?" I would ask. "Is he not a good man?" "I can't tell you why, but I just don't like him," she would say. And it would not be long before we would find out he was a rascal. Women sometimes have certain premonitions, and it is a good thing, because it often saves them from being misled.

"For Adam was first formed, then Eve. And Adam was not deceived, but the woman being deceived was in the transgression." Adam was not deluded. It was not to Adam that the Devil said, "Yea, hath God said, Ye shall not eat of every tree in the garden?" (Gen. 3:1). Satan said that to the woman. Her trouble was that she dilly-dallied with the Devil. She should have said, "It is not for me to say what I heard the Lord say to my husband. Go to him, and he will tell you." But she did not do that. She undertook to act for herself. Adam was not deceived, but the woman was deceived. I take it that Adam got into the transgression out of love for Eve. His heart was with her, and he determined that he would rather be with her in the place of disapproval than to be alone without her in a wonderful place of blessing. Adam went into it with his eyes open, and so he had to leave the garden of delight and go into the cold world.

After the fall God put upon Eve the curse of pain in travail: "In sorrow thou shalt bring forth children" (Gen. 3:16). But we read here in 1 Timothy, "Notwithstanding she shall be saved in childbearing, if they continue in faith and charity and holiness with sobriety." The Greek has "*the* childbearing." Many have taken it that this means as the woman brought sin into the world she shall be saved through the Lord Jesus Christ who was born of a woman. It is a rather difficult passage. On the other hand, there seems to be a great deal of comfort here for prospective parents. I cannot help but believe that this has reference to the hour of her trial, when she shall be preserved in childbearing, "If they continue in the faith [with love] and holiness with sobriety." I cannot quite fit the last part of this verse with salvation by grace if we think of it only as the incarnation. I think it has reference to the bringing of children into the world and the preservation of the mother at such a time, provided the husband and wife together continue in the faith with godliness and sobriety.

In this passage God puts before us the consistent Christian woman—and what a testimony for God is such a woman in the world today! I do not know of anyone whose influence counts more than that of a godly woman. It counts with her husband, the children, and with all those with whom she has to do. I do not know of anything that puts a greater reflection on Christianity than a careless, slothful, vain, carnal woman professing to be a Christian.

CHAPTER 7

Qualifications for Office in the Church

1 Timothy 3:1–13

We need to recognize the fact that Scripture distinguishes between gift and office. Our risen, glorified Lord, we are told, has given gifts unto men. "He gave some, apostles; and some, prophets; and some, evangelists; and some, pastors and teachers" (Eph. 4:11). These are divinely-given gifts for the edification of the church. It is God Himself who qualifies men for any of these particular lines of service. A man is not an evangelist because he goes to some school and develops a set technique and methods of preaching. A man is not necessarily a teacher of the Word because he takes some course of Bible instruction and then endeavors to pass on to others that which he has learned. But the risen Christ, by the Holy Spirit, qualifies men to do the work which He has for them. Never in Scripture do we have the least intimation that a man has to be humanly ordained in order that he may preach the gospel or teach the Word. We do not get anything like that in the Bible. It is the Lord Himself who gives the gifts. When He imparts the gift of preaching or teaching to any man, then the recipient is responsible to use his gift to the glory of the Lord Jesus Christ.

Some of the most widely used ministers of the gospel that have ever lived were never ordained by man. Charles H. Spurgeon, pastor for many years of the great Metropolitan Tabernacle in London, England, and one of the most outstanding Baptist preachers of his day, absolutely refused to be ordained by man. He utterly repudiated anything of the kind, saying the Lord Himself had ordained him and that was sufficient. D. L. Moody was never ordained by man, yet was a mighty evangelist who won thousands to Christ.

In Timothy's own case there was undoubtedly some formal service participated in by Paul and the elders of Derbe and Lystra before he went forth with the Apostle in itinerant missionary work. This is generally spoken of as his ordination, and perhaps it is correct to so speak, but actually it was more in the nature of a commendation and expression of fellowship. In response to the prayers and the laying on of hands of Paul and the elders on that occasion, God gave to Timothy a special gift to qualify him for the ministry he was to perform.

In the present section of our epistle, 3:1–13, Paul gives by inspiration the qualifications for official position in the local church. The officers may or may not be men of special gift. They must be men of sincere piety and exemplary lives. Verses 1–7 have to do with the selection of bishops, or overseers, and verses 8–13 with that of deacons, or servants.

Scripture recognizes these two offices in the church. Bishops and elders are one and the same, as a careful examination of certain passages will show.

"This is a true saying, If a man desire the office of a bishop, he desireth a good work." We see both offices in the book of Acts and also in the Epistles, and these elders and deacons are definitely appointed by the church. In the case of elders they were ordained by the apostles or by apostolic authority. The word *ordained* does not necessarily mean all that we sometimes put into it. We read, "Ye know the house of Stephanas, that it is the firstfruits of Achaia, and that they have addicted themselves to the ministry of the saints" (1 Cor. 16:15). The word rendered "addicted" is the same as that rendered "ordained" elsewhere.

First then notice what is said of those who are called bishops.

> This is a true saying, if a man desire the office of a bishop, he desireth a good work. A bishop then must be blameless, the husband of one wife, vigilant, sober, of good behaviour, given to hospitality, apt to teach; not given to wine, no striker, not greedy of filthy lucre; but patient, not a brawler, not covetous; one that ruleth well his own house, having his children in subjection with all gravity; (for if a man know not how to rule his own house, how shall he take care of the church of God?) Not a novice, lest being lifted up with pride he fall into the condemnation

> of the devil. Moreover he must have a good report of them which are without; lest he fall into reproach and the snare of the devil. (vv. 1–7)

"This is a true saying, if a man desire the office of a bishop, he desireth a good work." The word translated "bishop" means "overseer." If we turn to the epistle to Titus, we see that an elder and bishop are one and the same, "For this cause left I thee in Crete, that thou shouldest set in order the things that are wanting, and ordain elders in every city, as I had appointed thee: . . . For a bishop must be blameless, as the steward of God; not selfwilled, not soon angry, not given to wine, no striker, not given to filthy lucre" (1:5, 7). You see the Apostle is saying to Titus, "Now Titus, in order to complete the organization of the churches in Crete, you go from church to church and select out of the fellowship of your brethren suitable men to be ordained as elders in each of these churches." Then he gives the qualifications of a bishop. In verse 5 the word *elders* is used, and in verse 7 they are called *bishops. Elders* implies they are to be men of mature years. But the other term *bishops* means that they are to be competent to bear rule in the church of God.

You will never find anything like the modern bishop in the Bible. A bishop today, both in the Roman Catholic Church and in other churches which came out of Rome, is one of superior rank set in authority over other ministers. But there is no such idea as that in Scripture. In Acts 20 we find a number of bishops in one church, instead of one bishop set over many churches. In verse 17 the Apostle is addressing the elders of the church, and in verse 28 he says to them, "Take heed therefore unto yourselves, and to all the flock, over the which the Holy Ghost hath made you overseers, to feed the church of God, which he hath purchased with his own blood." The word *overseers* is a translation of the same word rendered *bishops,* so he says to these elders that they are to take care of the flock of God over which the Holy Spirit has made them bishops.

A great many things have come into the professing church for which there is no warrant in Scripture but which people take for granted. In certain organizations you have first a lower order of clergy called deacons, then a higher order called elders, and the highest of all called bishops. Some recognize even a higher order than these called archbishops, and then a few are selected from the archbishops, given red hats, and called cardinals. All that came in as a result of the church's departure from its early simplicity and of its imitation of the ways of the pagan systems.

What we need to keep in mind is that elders and bishops are one and the same. In the local church these are responsible for the spiritual affairs of the church, and we learn here the type of men that should be selected for this office.

Go back to verse 2: "A bishop then must be blameless, the husband of one wife." Do not misunderstand. The Apostle does not mean that a bishop must be sinless. If so, we could not have any bishops. Charles Spurgeon said a certain man whom he knew at one time was very pious. Mr. Spurgeon said he thought the man was practically sinless, until one day he said he was. Then Mr. Spurgeon knew he was not. A bishop must be a man of pure motives who desires to glorify our blessed Lord. He must be "blameless" as to motives. Then he is to be "the husband of one wife." It is amazing to think that in one of our great religious systems they hold that a clergyman of any character must have no wife. Scripture distinctly states that a bishop is to be "the husband of one wife, vigilant, sober, of good behaviour, given to hospitality, apt to teach." Those who hold the office of bishop are to be men who are interested in showing forth to others the grace of God in their Christian testimony. And, if God gives them a special gift, they are to use that gift in teaching the Word, not depending upon stimulants for inspiration but upon the Holy Spirit of God. They are to manifest a kindly interest in their brethren and in all men: "no striker," not one who readily loses his temper; "not a brawler," not quarrelsome; "not covetous," or a lover of money.

"One that ruleth well his own house, having his children in subjection with all gravity; (for if a man know not how to rule his own house, how shall he take care of the church of God?)." This is a very important qualification. We have often seen men aspiring to this office in the church whose children were a disgrace to them because of their willfulness and worldly ways. But the man who is fitted to have oversight in the church of God is one who has proven his ability to shepherd others by the way he rules his own household.

"Not a novice [not a new convert], lest being lifted up with pride he fall into the condemnation of the devil." The Devil fell through pride. He was created a glorious angel, Lucifer, but his heart was lifted up with pride, and because of that he rebelled against God and fell. He who was one of the anointed cherubim of the throne of God is now "that old serpent, the devil, and Satan." So the Apostle warns of the danger of selecting one who has been converted recently, and putting him in the special position of bishop, lest he be lifted up with pride.

"Moreover he must have a good report of them which are without; lest he fall into reproach and the snare of the devil." Men chosen for bishops are to be of such character that even the people of the world can look up to them and see in them what Christians ought to be.

> Likewise must the deacons be grave, not doubletongued, not given to much wine, not greedy of filthy lucre; holding the mystery of the

> faith in a pure conscience. And let these also first be proved; then let them use the office of a deacon, being found blameless. Even so must their wives be grave, not slanderers, sober, faithful in all things. Let the deacons be the husbands of one wife, ruling their children and their own houses well. For they that have used the office of a deacon well purchase to themselves a good degree, and great boldness in the faith which is in Christ Jesus. (vv. 8–13)

Here we have the qualifications of a deacon. The word *deacon* really means "servant," or "minister," and a deacon is to take care of the temporal affairs of the church of God. All who are deacons do not bear the title. For instance, a treasurer is a deacon, ushers are deacons, the men who look after the building, the trustees, are all deacons according to the Word of God. In Acts 6 we read of the first deacons. Seven men of honest report were chosen to take care of the distribution of the funds and the ministering to the poor and needy saints of Jerusalem. The word rendered "ministration" in Acts 6:1 is *diakonia.* Those who attended to this work were deacons, therefore.

In Romans 16 we find the feminine word for deacon. The Apostle sent his letter to the Romans by the hand of a lady who was traveling to Rome, and he calls her "Phebe our sister, which is a servant of the church which is at Cenchrea" (Rom. 16:1), literally, "a deaconess of the church at Cenchrea." She served the church. So a woman who serves the church is called, in Scripture, a "deaconess."

Deacons must "be grave," not given to frivolity, but realizing the seriousness of the work they are to undertake. "Not doubletongued"—one who will say one thing to one person and the opposite to someone else is double tongued. A deacon must be a man whose words can be depended upon. "Not given to much wine," not exhilarated by stimulants. "Not greedy of filthy lucre," not men who are seeking to enrich themselves.

"Holding the mystery of the faith in a pure conscience. And let these also first be proved; then let them use the office of a deacon, being found blameless." That is, they must be converted men, who, having received Christ, are faithful to the truth of God and obey His Word, ever seeking to maintain a pure conscience.

Next the Apostle mentions the wives of the deacons. Inasmuch as the deacons have to do with the temporal affairs of the church, their wives are likely to cause endless trouble unless they are wise, godly women. If the wife is a busybody she can destroy very easily her husband's influence for good. So the Apostle says, "Even so must their wives be grave, not slanderers, sober, faithful in all things." The word for "slanderers" is the plural for "devil"—that is, "she-devil." The Devil is the great slanderer. And the deacon's wife must be one who is not characterized by anything like that. "Sober, faithful in all things." A wife like this is a great asset to any man.

Reverting to the deacons, Paul says, "Let the deacons be the husbands of one wife, ruling their children and their own houses well." You get the same qualifications for those in charge of the temporal affairs of the church as for those who oversee its spiritual affairs. They must be men who maintain good order in their own houses.

Then in verse 13 he has a very nice thing to say for the encouragement of the deacons, "They that have used the office of a deacon well purchase to themselves a good degree, and great boldness in the faith which is in Christ Jesus." In other words, they who have delighted to serve the people of God, they who have had a real heart interest in the work of the church to the glory of God, they that have used their office unselfishly and faithfully "purchase to themselves a good degree, and great boldness in the faith which is in Christ Jesus."

We have that illustrated in a very remarkable way in the early chapters of the book of Acts. Among the seven deacons appointed on the occasion to which we have referred already were Stephen and Philip. Not long after Stephen's appointment as deacon we find him being led out by the Spirit of God to preach the Word and going from synagogue to synagogue in Jerusalem, proclaiming the truth that Jesus was the Christ. He had used well his office as a deacon. He had purchased to himself a good degree, and he was honored by becoming the first martyr who laid down his life for Christ's sake. Philip also used well his office of a deacon. Later on we learn that he went down to Samaria and there preached the Word, and many of the Samaritans believed and were baptized. He became known as an evangelist. It was he who was used to bring the gospel to the Ethiopian treasurer of Queen Candace. And in later years we find Philip in Cesarea maintaining a testimony for God.

We may not all hold official position, but we are all to serve according to the gift given by the grace of God, and we are responsible to be faithful in whatsoever place the Lord has set us. But those chosen or recognized by their brethren as fit to be trusted with special responsibilities in the church need special grace for the work they have to do.

CHAPTER 8

THE MYSTERY OF GODLINESS

1 Timothy 3:14–16

> These things write I unto thee, hoping to come unto thee shortly: but if I tarry long, that thou mayest know how thou oughtest to behave thyself in the house of God, which is the church of the living God, the pillar and ground of the truth. And without controversy great is the mystery of godliness: God was manifest in the flesh, justified in the Spirit, seen of angels, preached unto the Gentiles, believed on in the world, received up into glory. (vv. 14–16)

These words immediately follow instruction given as to the appointment of certain brethren for official position in the church of God. The Apostle was hoping to rejoin Timothy, but in the meantime, by divine inspiration, he wrote: "These things write I unto thee, hoping to come unto thee shortly: but if I tarry long, that thou mayest know how thou oughtest to behave thyself in the house of God, which is the church of the living God, the pillar and ground of the truth." Now Paul was not telling Timothy how to act when he went to church! Timothy was not a mere child who had to be instructed as to his behavior among a congregation gathered to worship God.

When the Apostle uses the expression "house of God," he is not referring to a material building. Men may speak of a building dedicated to the worship and praise of God as "the house of God," and there is a sense in which it is perfectly correct to so speak. It is important that Sunday school teachers and those who have the instruction of children impress upon their hearts the necessity of reverent behavior when they come into the building that has been set apart as a place where we come together to worship and sing praises to God, to lift up our voices in prayer, and for the ministry of His holy Word. It is most unbecoming for boys and girls—little ones and older ones, too—to be running around through the halls, giving vent to loud laughter, and various noises that disturb and distress others. We should realize that there is a certain demeanor that should characterize us when we enter such a building.

We Protestants have much to learn as to this from Roman Catholic and other ritualistic churches. They would not think of permitting their children to run around noisily through the building which they consider most sacred. Neither would they give themselves to loud conversation, or even whispering that disturbs those who are gathered to worship God. I think we should be concerned about these things. One of the crying evils of our generation is that of irreverence or lack of respect for the things of God.

But when the Apostle used the expression "the house of God," he was not referring to a material building. The "house of God" with him is the church of the living God, a spiritual building, made up of all those who are born of God, who are indwelt by the Holy Spirit, "in whom ye also are builded together for an habitation of God through the Spirit" (Eph. 2:22). Again and again, both in Paul's epistles and Peter's first epistle, the church of God is looked upon as being made up of living stones cemented together by the Holy Spirit, and in that building God dwells. We need to learn how we ought to conduct ourselves as members of the assembly of saints; how we ought to behave "in the house of God, which is the church of the living God, the pillar and ground [bulwark] of the truth." The only way we can learn this is through the study of the Scriptures, which tell us of the behavior that should characterize those who have faith in the Lord Jesus Chris, and recognize Him as Head of the body, the church.

This church is the pillar and ground or foundation of the truth. A pillar is for display purposes; the foundation is that on which the superstructure rests. The church was intended by our blessed Lord to be the pillar proclaiming the gospel of His grace while resting on the great foundation truths of the Word of God. We have no right to play fast and loose with revealed truth. We may be liberal with that which belongs to us, but this is God's truth, and we are to stand firmly for the faith once for all delivered to the saints.

In the next verse the Apostle speaks of the mystery of godliness, or, as it might be rendered, the secret of piety. When the children of Israel marched through the wilderness from Sinai on to the Promised Land, they carried with them the ark of the covenant which typified the Person of our Lord Jesus Christ—the meeting place between God and men. We today are responsible to maintain this sacred truth concerning our blessed Lord to which the Apostle refers as the mystery of godliness. The term *mystery* does not necessarily mean something which is, in itself, mysterious, but a secret revealed only to initiates. It is the will of God that the church should understand this secret, should know the truth concerning the Person of our Savior. This mystery is that of the incarnation—that God came down to earth, taking into union with His Deity a human body, a human spirit, and a human soul, so that He was both God and Man in one blessed, adorable Person.

"God was manifest in the flesh." Some of the early manuscripts omit "God" and render it "the mystery of godliness: which was manifest in the flesh." That is probably more correct than the later manuscripts, but the thought is clear that it was God Himself who came down into this scene and was manifested in the flesh. Jesus is both God and Man.

We read in the gospel of John, "No man hath seen God at any time, the only begotten Son, which is in the bosom of the Father, he hath declared him" (1:18) or, "told Him out." Again we read, "The Word was made flesh, and dwelt among us, (and we beheld his glory, the glory as of the only begotten of the Father,) full of grace and truth" (John 1:14). And so "God was in Christ, reconciling the world unto himself, not imputing their trespasses unto them" (2 Cor. 5:19).

In the second place we read that He was "justified in the Spirit." He who was God manifest in the flesh was absolutely the righteous One conceived without sin. After His baptism in the Jordan, where He publicly dedicated Himself as the One who had come to fulfill all righteousness and so to settle the sin question, God the Father opened the heavens above Him, the Holy Spirit descended upon Him, and the Father's voice was heard declaring, "This is my beloved Son, in whom I am well pleased" (Matt. 3:17); or, "in whom I have found all My delight." Thus He was justified in the Spirit. There was no taint of sin in Him. He was absolutely holy. As such He was the suited Substitute to take the sinner's place and to endure the judgment that our sins deserved.

In the third place—and this is to me most interesting—we read, He was "seen of angels." He is called elsewhere "the Image of the invisible God." Did you ever stop to think of this? Before God became incarnate in Jesus Christ He was invisible to created eyes. God the Father was invisible; God the Son was invisible; God the Holy Spirit was invisible. Angels could look only upon the glory of God but could not see the invisible One. But when the Lord Jesus

Christ came down to earth, when the Babe was born in Bethlehem's manger, He who was God from all eternity had become visible. As angels hung over that crib and gazed upon the face of that little Babe, they knew they were looking into the face of the God who had created them. As He walked on earth angels were beholding the wondrous works wrought by God manifest in flesh. And you and I shall see Him in all the blessed reality of His Manhood as well as His Deity throughout all eternity.

"Preached unto the Gentiles." The word rendered "Gentiles" is the word elsewhere translated "nations"—that is, the time had come when God no longer was to have one people separated from the rest of the nations, but His love could go out to all mankind. So our Lord Jesus Christ is preached unto all nations. The message preached to the nations everywhere is that all may be saved who will turn to Him in faith.

Next we read, He was "believed on in the world." After twenty centuries there are untold millions in unbelief. In fact, there are millions who have never heard His name. That ought to stir our hearts to increased missionary activity and missionary giving. But even among those who have heard His name there are vast throngs who refuse to trust Him. But, thank God, all through the centuries since the cross vast numbers have believed. Today millions believe on Him and find in Him not only a Savior, not only the One who gives comfort and rest to their consciences, but they find also a loving, tender Friend who gives peace to the heart in the midst of the perplexities and toils of life. To believe on Him is to put your trust in Him, to claim Him as your own personal Savior.

Last of all we read, He was "received up into glory." Paul was not giving a chronological account of the incarnation and life of our Lord Jesus Christ, but he was bringing out one truth after another in the measure of its importance. He who left the Father's house came down to earth where He lived a sinless life. He who was the absolutely holy and spotless One went to the cross to die for our sins. He who was preached unto the Gentiles and who has been believed on in the world, He, the Man Christ Jesus, has been received up into glory. He is the very same Person in heaven today that He was when He was here on earth.

Many seem to have the idea that after the ascension of our Lord He ceased to be the Man Christ Jesus and became some kind of a spiritual being, so that they imagine they will never see Him as He was when He left this scene and returned to the Father. But the angels on Mount Olivet said to the disciples, "Why stand ye gazing up into heaven? this same Jesus, which is taken up from you into heaven, shall so come in like manner as ye have seen him go into heaven" (Acts 1:11). He is absolutely unchangeable: "The same yesterday, and to day, and for ever" (Heb. 13:8).

When we behold Him we will know Him by the print of the nails in His hand. When He descends the second time to take His kingdom and appear to His own people Israel, their eyes will be open to recognize Him. They will say to Him, "What are these wounds in thine hands? Then he shall answer, Those with which I was wounded in the house of my friends" (Zech. 13:6). When at last we look up into His blessed face, we will see the marks of the thorny crown. As He lifts those loving hands, we will behold the scars left by the wounds, and we will say, "This is my Lord and my God," even as Thomas said when he fell down in worship at the Savior's feet.

CHAPTER 9

The Latter Days

1 Timothy 4:1–6

> Now the Spirit speaketh expressly, that in the latter times some shall depart from the faith, giving heed to seducing spirits, and doctrines of devils; speaking lies in hypocrisy; having their conscience seared with a hot iron; forbidding to marry, and commanding to abstain from meats, which God hath created to be received with thanksgiving of them which believe and know the truth. For every creature of God is good, and nothing to be refused, if it be received with thanksgiving: for it is sanctified by the word of God and prayer. If thou put the brethren in remembrance of these things, thou shalt be a good minister of Jesus Christ, nourished up in the words of faith and of good doctrine, whereunto thou hast attained. (vv. 1–6)

It is a remarkable fact that our blessed Lord and His apostles indicated, before they left this scene, the decadence of the very system which they came to introduce, that is, they came to introduce what we commonly call Christianity. Yet both our Lord and His followers afterward warned the early church that there would be a great departure from the truth and that increasing apostasy would be manifest as the years wore on, until eventually there would be a complete turning away from the faith. Men would accept antichrist instead of the Christ of God.

As we look back over the centuries that have passed since apostolic days, we can see how literally these predictions have been fulfilled. All down through these centuries there has been increasing departure from the simplicity of the gospel. All kinds of false systems have come in, until there was a time when it seemed as though false teaching was the real thing, and the truth of God was looked upon as heresy. There has been a revival in the preaching of the gospel, however, for which we can be thankful to God.

Here the Apostle warns of a time of apostasy which was to come, as he intimates, "in the latter times." The "latter times" are to be distinguished from "the last days" described in 2 Timothy 3:1, "This know also, that in the last days perilous times shall come." There he depicts conditions that will prevail in the professing church immediately before the return of the Lord Jesus Christ—conditions which do prevail largely today throughout Christendom. But the period spoken of here in chapter 4 is called "the latter times." This period is for us in the past. We look back, not forward, to the latter times. The events described here have taken place already. They have been fulfilled already.

In 2 Thessalonians 2:7 we read, "For the mystery of iniquity doth already work." That is, vain, unscriptural teaching was even then beginning to permeate the church. Here Paul warns Timothy, and through Timothy all other believers, of some of the results of the condition that was to be manifested later on.

"Now the Spirit speaketh expressly." All prophecy is by the Holy Spirit. It is He alone who can foresee the future. It is not given to man to do this. Men may guess what the future may be, and sometimes their guesses may turn out to be correct, but no man can speak authoritatively as to the future. He does not know what the next day may bring forth. But the Spirit of God, looking down through the centuries of time, empowered certain of Christ's servants to predict many things that were to prevail long years ahead. In the Old Testament, a large portion is devoted to prophecy, but we also have prophecy in the New Testament. Here is an instance of the Spirit speaking expressly, "that in the latter times some shall depart from the faith, giving heed to seducing spirits, and doctrines of devils; speaking lies in hypocrisy; having their conscience seared with a hot iron."

You will notice there are three classes of personalities brought before us here. First we read of some who will depart from the faith; some who were nominal Christians, members of the professing church, but who would drift away from the truth as given by our Lord Jesus Christ and His inspired apostles. One needs only a slight acquaintance with church history to know how these words were fulfilled in what we call the "Dark" or "Middle Ages," but which the Roman Catholic Church calls the "Age of Faith," because those were the years in which people forsook the teachings of the Word of God and received the superstitious traditions of the Roman Church. They departed from the faith. They substituted the authority of the church for that of the Holy Scriptures.

The second class is called "seducing spirits," who propogate "doctrines of devils," or teachings of demons. These evil spirits are ever active in seeking to turn men away from the faith once for all delivered to the saints. They are in rebellion against God, and yet are permitted for some strange, mysterious reason to influence and even possess men and women who are not subject to the instruction of the Holy Spirit. They are led by their prince, Beelzebub, and are actively engaged in combating the faith of Christ.

Then there is a third class. We might not realize this from our King James Version, but the translation made by that great Greek scholar, William Kelly, reads: "Some shall fall away from the faith, giving heed to seducing spirits, and teachings of demons by hypocrisy of the legend-mongers." That is the way evil teaching was to be presented to men, "through the hypocrisy of legend-mongers"—men who substituted legends for the truth of God. We look back through the centuries and see that these came in very early.

There were not many copies of Scripture available during the Middle Ages, and the great majority of Christians did not have even a part of the Bible, nor would they have been able to read it if they had possessed it. The few manuscripts that were available were generally in the hands of teachers. Many of them were kept in monasteries. And so it was easy for interested persons to foist legends and traditions upon the common people in place of the inspired revelation which God had given. Many such legends were promulgated in those dark ages.

It is amazing, as we look back, to see how ready people were to accept all kinds of myths rather than the precious gospel as made known in the Bible. One legend was that of the Immaculate Conception of the Virgin Mary, the teaching that she was born without sin, and so in that sense she was like her Son, the Lord Jesus Christ Himself. Another legend that was foisted upon the people was that Mary never actually died, but was taken up into heaven, crowned, and today reigns as queen of heaven. The legend of purgatory was substituted as a place of cleansing from sin instead of the precious blood of our Lord Jesus Christ alone. Many others came in and similarly nullified the plain teaching of Holy Scriptures. They were accepted as though of the same authority as God's Holy Word, and so brought men's hearts into bondage.

Those who were Satan's agents in vending these legends, instead of the truth of the gospel, are said to have "their conscience seared with a hot iron." They reached the place where conscience no longer responded to the voice of God. Notice the contrast between these and those who stood for the truth in verse 9 of the previous chapter. The Apostle speaks of Christians as "holding the mystery of the faith in a pure conscience." The people of whom he is speaking in verse 2 of this fourth chapter turn away from the faith and accept false theories and invalid legends. They are said to have their consciences seared with a hot iron. They became utterly calloused.

In the next verse we read of certain manifest signs that help us to identify the persons whom the Spirit of God has in mind when He speaks so solemnly here. "Forbidding to marry, and commanding to abstain from meats, which God hath created to be received with thanksgiving of them which believe and know the truth." Here are two outward things that would make it very easy for anyone to understand, when the time came, who and of what the apostle Paul was speaking as he wrote by inspiration of the Holy Spirit.

It was during those dark ages that an apostate church arose which taught that a celibate priest or monk was a holier person than the Christian father or husband, and an unmarried nun was on a higher moral plane than a godly wife or mother, and so certain ones were forbidden to marry. Now Scripture maintains that there are occasions when it is better to remain unmarried. For instance, if Christian workers are exposed to great dangers, it is far better not to think of marrying and dragging wives and possibly children into such circumstances. But God Himself instituted marriage for a holy purpose. Men attempting to be wiser than God put the ban upon marriage, so that certain persons who were separated from the world as nuns, monks, and priests had to take a vow not to marry. By this we may see to whom the Apostle was referring here.

Then observe the next mark: "Commanding to abstain from meats." Now our Lord Jesus Christ Himself told us, "Not that which goeth into the mouth defileth a man; but that which cometh out of the mouth, this defileth a man" (Matt. 15:11). But there soon grew up in the professing church the notion that the eating of meat on certain days should be refrained from because by so doing one could better master the desires of the flesh—a theory which has proven to be false. Men are still as sinful as before. Vegetarianism has never worked for greater holiness than the ordinary method of nourishing the body, which is according to God's own order. But men cannot seem to get away from this outward thing, which is the teaching of demons.

In *Foxe's Book of Martyrs* an incident is related of a man who was to be burned at the stake because he would not bow down before a wafer and worship it as

God incarnate. The wood bundles were piled around him, and the executioner was waiting to put the torch to them. A priest stood on a high platform nearby and preached a sermon. He took for a text the first two verses of this chapter: "Now the Spirit speaketh expressly, that in the latter times some shall depart from the faith, giving heed to seducing spirits, and doctrines of devils; speaking lies in hypocrisy; having their conscience seared with a hot iron." These words he applied to the martyr about to die as a condemned heretic. Having finished the sermon, the priest said, "Have you anything to say before you are burned? Will you recant and receive the absolution of the church?" The man, looking up, replied, "I have nothing to say except that I wish you would read aloud the next verse following the two you have read." The priest looked at the passage: "Forbidding to marry, and commanding to abstain from meats, which God hath created to be received with thanksgiving of them which believe and know the truth." Instead of reading it he gave the signal to put the torch to the wood, and then he threw the Testament into the fire. It was too much. It condemned him, and showed exactly where the evil was, and what was meant by the Holy Spirit when He spoke of the doctrine of demons to be made known in the latter times.

This evil system which began in the latter times is prevalent today all over Christendom, and there is a definite line drawn between the Holy Scriptures and these superstitions that have been foisted upon people as inspired and authoritative traditions. We ought to thank God for the open Bible, where truth is found so crystal clear!

The Apostle adds, "For every creature of God is good, and nothing to be refused, if it be received with thanksgiving." I wonder if we are as conscientious as we should be about giving thanks to God for the good things He has provided. It is shocking to notice Christians who sit down in public eating places and give no evidence that they have thanked God for what is before them. Perhaps they do thank Him silently, but do not let those around them realize it. Christians, wherever you are when you partake of food you should be careful to honor God by giving thanks. Many opportunities will arise to speak to needy souls, even at the same table or at a table nearby, if you bow your head in a restaurant or hotel and give thanks before partaking of your food. Christians should never sit down to a table at home without giving thanks for that which God has spread before them. Yet I am afraid many of us fail even in this.

On the other hand, I have seen people sit down to a table and it may be that the husband will give thanks, and but within a few minutes he begins to fuss and growl about the food, complaining about it. Perhaps the poor wife has done her best, and that is all the thanks she gets! If we receive the food with thanksgiving then we should not complain about it. After all, no matter how poor it is, it is still too good for sinners. Had God treated us according to our deserts we would be in the pit of woe, forever beyond the reach of mercy.

"Sanctified by the word of God and prayer." What a blessed thing it is when the Word of God is honored and the voice of prayer ascends to heaven as the family gathers about the table to enjoy the good things the Lord has provided. Many of us look back on such scenes of family worship, and how we thank God for the impressions made upon our hearts and lives in early days.

"If thou put the brethren in remembrance of these things, thou shalt be a good minister of Jesus Christ, nourished up in the words of faith and of good doctrine [or healthful teaching], whereunto thou hast attained." The minister of Christ is responsible to bring these things to bear upon the hearts and consciences of the people of God, in order that He may be honored and they may be preserved from the unholy teachings which Satan uses to lead many astray.

CHAPTER 10

Practical Godliness

1 Timothy 4:7–16

> But refuse profane and old wives' fables, and exercise thyself rather unto godliness. For bodily exercise profiteth little: but godliness is profitable unto all things, having promise of the life that now is, and of that which is to come. This is a faithful saying and worthy of all acceptation. For therefore we both labour and suffer reproach, because we trust in the living God, who is the Saviour of all men, specially of those that believe. These things command and teach. Let no man despise thy youth; but be thou an example of the believers, in word, in conversation, in charity, in spirit, in faith, in purity. Till I come, give attendance to reading, to exhortation, to doctrine. Neglect not the gift that is in thee, which was given thee by prophecy, with the laying on of the hands of the presbytery. Meditate upon these things; give thyself wholly to them; that thy profiting may appear to all. Take heed unto thyself, and unto the doctrine; continue in them: for in doing this thou shalt both save thyself, and them that hear thee. (vv. 7–16)

In this particular section of the epistle, the Apostle dwells upon godliness in the life, particularly in the life of a minister of Christ for he was addressing the young preacher Timothy whom he had left in Ephesus, in order that he might help the church there.

Now no man can lift another person above his own level. If a minister of Christ is going to be used of God in reaching and elevating others, he must be characterized by true piety himself. Paul knew Timothy and knew what kind of man he was. He writes in other places commending him earnestly as one who had been as a son to him in his service for the Lord. Nevertheless, he felt it necessary to stir up the heart of Timothy to the importance of living wholly for God. But as we study these words, we should not think of them as applying only to one in full-time service for Christ. There is a sense in which all Christians are called upon to be ministers of Christ, for a minister is a servant, and we are all looked upon as servants of the One who has redeemed us. We are to be occupied in seeking to make Him known to others as far as we possibly can.

In the first place, Paul says to Timothy, "But refuse profane and old wives' fables." How much this admonition is needed today! "Profane and old wives' fables"—that is, things that are opposed to the truth of God, imaginary ideas, such as ignorant old women devoid of spiritual insight might be inclined to circulate. Have you ever noticed that a great number of modern teachings which are leading people astray are but old wives' fables? Both Madame Blavatsky and Mrs. Annie Besant, the cofounders of theosophy, were "old wives" whose fables have deceived thousands. Mrs. Ellen G. White's fantastic "sanctuary theory," the basic doctrine of Seventh-day Adventism, is an old wife's fable. Mary Baker Patterson Glover Eddy was an old wife, who mothered what she falsely called "Christian Science."

These teachings are all contrary to the truth of God. Such have a special attraction for women of a particular type. And so Paul warns Timothy against all such perversions of truth. He says, "Exercise thyself rather unto godliness." *Godliness* is just a clipped word. It was originally "Godlikeness" and so is rendered in some of the older English translations (Wycliffe has *Gudlyknesse.*) Godliness is genuine piety. That is its real meaning.

No one will live a truly pious life who neglects the means which God has given to us for this purpose. We have the Word of God; we need to study our Bibles. And we need to take much time for prayer. Then we must be faithful in testifying to those who are unsaved. To honor God in these things is to be exercised unto godliness.

"For bodily exercise profiteth little." There are three different ways in which this clause might be read. As rendered in the King James Version, we might understand it to mean that bodily exercise is not of very great profit because life is so short, and eternal things are so much more important. John Wesley renders it, "Bodily exercise profiteth *a* little"—that is, somewhat, but not to be compared with exercise unto godliness. Others read it, "Bodily exercise profiteth *for a little time*"—the time we are going through this world. "But godliness is profitable unto all things, having promise of the life that now is, and of that which is to come." I would stress this and seek to impress it upon the hearts of all who are young in Christ.

My younger brethren and sisters, you who have strong, healthy bodies, you naturally and rightfully delight to indulge in certain physical exercises. But oh, let me press this upon your minds: just as these things have a place in the physical realm, it is far more important that you be strong spiritually. Do not neglect your soul as you care for your body. Do not be so much concerned about bodily exercise that you fail to take plenty of time over the Word of God and in prayer that you may be strong, healthy Christians, whose lives will bring the approval of the blessed Lord at His judgment seat. Godliness is profitable all through this life. And oh, how profitable will it prove to have been when we leave this world and go out into eternity! After all, life is so short it seems a terrible mistake to devote the greater part of our time to concern for the things of this life while forgetting the important things of eternity.

I was somewhat acquainted with C. J. Baker, the father-in-law of Dr. Walter Wilson. He was a fine Christian businessman, head of a large firm in Kansas City which manufactured tents and awnings of all descriptions. He sold his merchandise very largely to circus and Chautauqua people. Every year he sent forth his catalog, knowing that it would be read by many unconverted showmen and others. I recall a greeting he had placed upon the first page: "With our best wishes to our customers for time and eternity, especially eternity." It was signed, "C. J. Baker." I often wondered what the reaction would be as these unsaved people received that catalog from that Christian man who expressed such concern for their welfare, not only in this life but also in the life which is to come! That is what really counts. Godliness is profitable, not only for this life but also for that which is to come.

Next, we have another "faithful saying." In 1:15 we read, "This is a faithful saying, and worthy of all acceptation, that Christ Jesus came into the world to save sinners; of whom I am chief." Now in 4:9–10 we have a faithful saying for the people of God: "This is a faithful saying and worthy of all acceptation. For therefore we both labour and suffer reproach, because we trust in the living God, who is the Saviour of all men, specially of those that believe." This, you see, is for those who know the Lord, those who found out they were sinners and came to Christ and have been saved by His grace. How we should delight to labor and suffer reproach for His sake! We know how wonderfully God takes care of His own. But He "is the Saviour of all men." He is watching over all mankind, but especially is He the Savior of those who believe.

Then Paul says to Timothy, "These things command and teach." Timothy was a young man. Perhaps by this time he may have been about forty years of age, but a man of forty was comparatively young compared with Paul who perhaps at this time was close to seventy. So he writes to the younger man, "Let no man despise thy youth." That is, do not develop an inferiority complex because you are younger than some of those to whom you minister. Do not be concerned if they do not understand that God has called you to this position, and if they seek to ignore you because of your comparative immaturity.

"But be thou an example of the believers, in word, in conversation [that is, behavior], in charity, in spirit, in faith, in purity." A young man may be very immature in some respects, but if he is characterized by these things: careful as to his words, particular as to his behavior, and manifesting the love of God; if he is a man of faith and is careful as to purity of life, he will not have to try to compel others to accord him recognition. His behavior will accredit him to those to whom he ministers. They will realize that though a young man there is something about him that marks him out as a man of God, and not one who is careless in his walk and slack in his service, or who is seeking an easygoing life as a professional cleric.

"Till I come, give attendance to reading, to exhortation, to doctrine." There are two different Greek words for "reading." One means to read to others; the other means to read for one's own instruction and information. It is the first word that is used here: "Till I come, give [attention] to reading"—that is, reading to others. On the other hand, may I add this: He who would be a faithful minister of Christ must take plenty of time to read for his own edification. He needs to read and meditate on the Scriptures and also such literature as God has provided in order to help him to better understand the Word. Having done this he can communicate to others the truth which has become precious to his own soul.

"Neglect not the gift that is in thee, which was given thee by prophecy, with the laying on of the hands of the presbytery." That word translated "presbytery" is generally rendered "elders." It is evident that the elders of the church at Lystra and Derbe had met together with the apostle Paul when Timothy was about to launch out in full-time service and had laid their hands on him, commending him to God in prayer. That is sometimes spoken of as Timothy's ordination. We do not read in Scripture that anyone has to be ordained to preach the gospel, but the laying on of hands was an expression of fellowship. As these brethren prayed for Timothy, God gave him a special gift. These elders were men of God. It is far otherwise in many instances.

Charles H. Spurgeon, who always refused human ordination, used to say that in many cases when men profess to have the authority to ordain another to preach or teach the gospel and pretend that through ordination they are enabled to give him some special gift, it is just "laying empty hands on an empty head!" But in Timothy's case these brethren prayed in faith, and God gave the answer. I rather think it was the gift of a pastor that was conferred upon Timothy.

"Meditate upon these things; give thyself wholly to them; that thy profiting may appear to all." No one who really wants to count for God can afford to play at Christianity. He must make it the one great business of his life. Whether he is set apart for special ministry—as a missionary who is going to a foreign land, a laborer in the gospel in home fields, or whether he remains in business and seeks to witness for Christ there—he needs to give himself entirely to a life of devotion to the Lord.

Notice the closing words: "Take heed unto thyself, and unto the doctrine." Observe the order: first, "take heed unto *thyself*"—be careful about your own inner and outward life, setting an example to others. Then take heed "unto the doctrine." We read of Ezra in the Old Testament who "prepared his heart to *seek* the law of the Lord, and to *do* it, and to *teach* in Israel statutes and judgments" (Ezra 7:10). Many people prepare the mind who do not prepare the heart, but Ezra put the heart first. He desired to know the law of God, and he learned it not only through the head but also through the heart. Then it says he "prepared his heart to seek the law of the Lord, and to do it." He was not going to teach others what he did not do himself. And so God used and honored a man like that.

That is the way He does today. "Take heed unto thyself, and unto the doctrine; continue in them: for in doing this thou shalt both save thyself, and them that hear thee." He is not speaking of the salvation of the soul. He is not referring to eternal salvation. But he is exhorting Timothy to be careful to live for God, to be a consistent, earnest minister of Christ, because in doing this he would both save himself and others from many snares and difficulties. He would become a blessing instead of a curse to those to whom he ministered.

No one can live a godly life who has not first received Christ as his own Savior. You cannot live a Christian life until you are born again. I would remind my reader of the words, "He that hath the Son hath life; and he that hath not the Son of God hath not life" (1 John 5:12). After Christ is known in this way we are prepared to lead others to Him and guide them in the path of obedience.

CHAPTER 11

The Church's Responsibility in Temporal Things

1 Timothy 5:1–16

Rebuke not an elder, but intreat him as a father; and the younger men as brethren; the elder women as mothers; the younger as sisters, with all purity. Honour widows that are widows indeed. But if any widow have children or nephews, let them learn first to show piety at home, and to requite their parents: for that is good and acceptable before God. Now she that is a widow indeed, and desolate, trusteth in God, and continueth in supplications and prayers night and day. But she that liveth in pleasure is dead while she liveth. And these things give in charge, that they may be blameless. But if any provide not for his own, and specially for those of his own house, he hath denied the faith, and is worse than an infidel. Let not a widow be taken into the number under threescore years old, having been the wife of one man, well reported of for good works; if she have brought up children, if she have lodged strangers, if she have washed the saints' feet, if she have relieved the afflicted, if she have diligently followed every good work. But the younger widows refuse: for when they have begun to wax wanton against Christ, they

> will marry; having damnation, because they have cast off their first faith. And withal they learn to be idle, wandering about from house to house; and not only idle, but tattlers also and busybodies, speaking things which they ought not. I will therefore that the younger women marry, bear children, guide the house, give none occasion to the adversary to speak reproachfully. For some are already turned aside after Satan. If any man or woman that believeth have widows, let them relieve them, and let not the church be charged; that it may relieve them that are widows indeed. (vv. 1–16)

We hear a great deal today in many quarters about the Social Gospel, and by that is meant the implication that the one great business of the church of God in the world is to try to better the temporal circumstances of those among whom it ministers. Many churches have given up, to a large extent, the preaching of the gospel of Christ in order to devote themselves to this Social Gospel. There should be no question as to the fact that from the earliest days of the church, immediately following Pentecost, Christians did recognize that they had a responsibility to those among them who were in need and distress. We are told in Galatians 6:10, "As we have therefore opportunity, let us do good unto all men, especially unto them who are of the household of faith." But our great business is to go into all the world and preach the gospel. The Lord Himself gives gifts to teach and preach that the church may be built up in the things of God.

As Christians go on with the Lord, they will recognize their duty toward those in less comfortable circumstances than themselves. In other passages of the New Testament we have emphasized for us our responsibility as Christians to think of the needy and the suffering.

I remember years ago when working among the Navaho Indians in the southwest down in Arizona and New Mexico, we were having a workers' conference at one time. There came out from the East a representative of one of the larger denominations which was given to a great extent to this so-called "Social Gospel." He was speaking one afternoon, and said that he had been shocked as he traveled over the reservation and saw something of the filth and poverty in which many of the Indians lived. Turning to one of the missionaries he said, "My brother, I think your first responsibility is to teach these people the use of soap and water and a toothbrush, and the use of vermin-destroying fluids of some kind or another. You will never be able to make Christians out of them until you show them how to improve their homes and teach them to value cleanliness and decency."

When the man sat down, one of the young Navaho preachers got up and said something like this: "I was very much interested in what our friend from the East had to say. I never thought our responsibility was to go about and preach a gospel of soap and water. I thought it was to carry the gospel of the cleansing blood of Christ. But after we get one of our Navaho people saved, if he has been used to living in filth, when we go back to visit him we find things are all changed. When they get cleaned up inside then they want things clean outside." He added, "I don't want to take issue with our friend who has come to visit us, but I think he is putting the cart before the horse when he insists on the Social Gospel first instead of the gospel of the grace of God."

Now that young Navaho was right. Many of us with years of experience have observed that there is nothing that changes the outward circumstances of people like having them get right with God in their hearts. But on the other hand, when we do get right with God, we ought to remember that we do have certain social responsibilities.

By the way, while I am speaking of this, let me add one other testimony to that of the Navaho. Many years ago when I was a Salvation Army officer we had gathered for an officers' council—that is what others would call a ministerial association—and General William Booth himself was addressing us. He talked about the social program that he had proposed in a book that had just then been published titled *In Darkest England and the Way Out.* General Booth said, "My Comrades, never allow yourselves to put social work before the gospel of the grace of God." Then to illustrate what he meant he said, "Take a man who has ruined himself by strong drink, has become a confirmed drunkard, beggared his family so that his wife has been separated from him, and his children are in orphan homes. He is just a common drunkard on the street. Take that man and sober him up, get him to sign the pledge and promise never to take another drink, move him out into the country in a new environment, settle him down in a little cottage, teach him a trade if he does not know one, bring back his wife and children, make his home a comfortable one, and then let him die in his sin and go to hell at last! Really it is not worthwhile, and I for one would not attempt it."

That was General Booth speaking. He was emphasizing the mistake of meeting the physical needs of people rather than the spiritual needs. First of all, get men right with God and other things will follow in due order.

In our epistle the Apostle is putting before Timothy some principles for the church of God. First we have three verses that deal with the matter of Christian courtesy. "Rebuke not an elder, but intreat him as a father; and the younger men as brethren; the elder women as mothers; the younger as sisters, with all purity.

Honour widows that are widows indeed." The Christian company was necessarily separated from the world without. When a person became a child of God in those days, he was soon outside the synagogue if a Jew and outside the fellowship of idolatry if a Gentile. These Christians were brought together in very intimate association, and their communion one with another was most precious and intense. But there is always the possibility that when people are thus linked together that they will forget that natural courtesy that should be shown to one another. The Spirit of God stresses the importance of this.

"Rebuke not an elder." I take it he does not mean an official elder, because he contrasts an elder man with a younger man. He means: Do not rebuke one advanced in years. If such an one needs a word of admonition, go to him in a kindly manner and speak to him as one would speak to a father. But never, as a young man, upbraid an older man, because if you do it will only show your own ill-breeding and your lack of subjection to the Spirit of God. Deal with younger men as brethren. Timothy was a preacher of the Word. He was to look at all younger men in the fellowship as brothers in Christ and treat them as such. He was not to take a place of authority among them, domineering over them, but he was to seek to work with them as on one common level and recognize them as brothers in Christ.

He was to esteem older women as he would his own mother. What a beautiful ideal! He was to look upon a lady who had grown old in the service of the Lord with the same reverent feeling that he would look upon the countenance of his own mother and be ready to help her in any way he could. He was to treat younger women as though they were his sisters, with all purity. That is, never to act toward any young woman in a way he would not like some other man to behave to his own sister.

Widows who had lost their companions and perhaps were left without any visible means of support were to be honored because of the place they held. Homes such as are in operation today to shelter those who have no means of support were not known at that time, and the church had a special responsibility toward the widows for whom no provision had been made. The church still has a definite duty to fulfill to those of its own who are left in poverty and distress because of the decease of their natural providers.

On the other hand, relatives are never to turn over the care of widows to the church if they, themselves, are able to look after these widows. "But if any widow have children or nephews [the word translated *nephews* really means "descendants"], let them learn first to show piety at home, and to requite their parents: for that is good and acceptable before God." If there is an aged sister left a widow and she has sons or daughters or other descendants, they are to understand that they are morally responsible to keep her. They are not to turn her over to some institution to look after her.

The Jews have a very interesting story that they tell of a young Jew who had the responsibility to care for his aged father. The young man married, and his wife was very proud and greatly resented having the care of her father-in-law in the home and having part of their money go to his support. So she was constantly nagging her husband, begging him to send the old gentleman to the Poor Farm. Finally the young man turned to his father and said, "Father, I shall have to take you to the Poor Farm." The old man wept and pleaded, saying, "My dear boy, I am already seventy-six years of age. Please care for me a few years or months longer. I don't want to die in the Poor Farm." But the young man said, "You will have to come with me." So he placed his hand on the old man's arm, and they started down the road. On they went, the young man dragging his father by force while the old gentleman complained until they got to a certain tree. Then the old man stopped and said, "No! No! No! I will not go any farther. I didn't drag my father any farther than this tree!" Is not the lesson plain?

If you are not gracious and kind to the old, the day may come when you yourself will be old and you will reap as you sow. We who can do so are to care for our older relatives. This is just ordinary Christianity in action.

"Now she that is a widow indeed, and desolate, trusteth in God, and continueth in supplications and prayers night and day." That is, one who has been bereft of her husband in advanced age and feels her loss, but trusts in God and spends much time before Him in prayer is a blessing to the entire Christian community to which she belongs.

On the other hand, there are some widows who seem almost glad to have their liberty, and when the husband is dead they rejoice in their freedom. They give themselves to folly and pleasure. So we read, "But she that liveth in pleasure is dead while she liveth." The church has no responsibility to support widows of that kind, and they themselves will have to answer to God for their careless behavior. Notice those words. They apply not only to careless widows but also to anyone else living in pleasure: "dead while she liveth!" The only right life is the life lived to the glory of God.

"And these things give in charge, that they may be blameless." Again the Apostle stresses the responsibility of those who have others dependent upon them.

"But if any provide not for his own, and specially for those of his own house, he hath denied the faith, and is worse than an infidel." That is a serious word for anyone who refuses to labor and properly take care of wife or children or others dependent upon him. No matter what kind of religious profession a man makes, he has denied the faith and is worse than an utter unbeliever if he neglects his family and leaves them in want when by proper care he could meet their needs.

In the early church certain arrangements were made to provide for these widows. We see this in the sixth chapter of Acts. You remember the first murmuring in the church occurred because of some of the widows of the Greek-speaking Jews complained that they were not as well cared for as the widows of the Palestinian Jews, and that led to the appointment of the seven deacons to handle the distribution of the funds for this purpose.

The Apostle says, "Let not a widow be taken into the number under threescore years old, having been the wife of one man, well reported of for good works; if she have brought up children, if she have lodged strangers, if she have washed the saints' feet, if she have relieved the afflicted, if she have diligently followed every good work." It was these things that entitled a widow to the charity of the church: sixty years of age, presumably unable to earn her own living, a consistent record in the past—that is, she cared for strangers when she had a husband and a home. "If she have washed the saints' feet." It was an Oriental way of saying, "If she has been hospitable." It was a custom in that time, when one wearing sandals entered a home, a servant would bring water, remove the sandals, and bathe the travel-worn feet of the visitor. If the widow had done all these things for the comfort and cheer of her guests, then she certainly was entitled to the care of the church in the time of her bereavement and poverty.

"But the younger widows refuse." They presumably were able to earn their own living. It was not expected that the church should assume responsibility toward them. If so, it would have encouraged them in idleness. They would not have found it necessary to become employed in any useful calling. "For when they have begun to wax wanton against Christ, they will marry." In this way they might have brought discredit upon the church of God. God said to Israel, "Why gaddest thou about so much to change thy way?" (Jer. 2:36). These young widows, if they had no responsibility, would be in danger of wandering about from house to house. Not only would they be idle, but they might also become tattlers and busybodies, carrying tales from one home to another. When people have nothing else to do they generally set their tongues working overtime. "The tongue is a little member, and boasteth great things" (James 3:5). To avoid idle gossip the younger widows should be gainfully employed.

"I will therefore that the younger women marry, bear children, guide the house, give none occasion to the adversary to speak reproachfully. For some are already turned aside after Satan." He had evidently heard of some in the church who had thus gone astray.

As he closes this section, Paul again points out the responsibility of the relatives to care for aging widows. "If any man or woman that believeth have widows, let them relieve them, and let not the church be charged; that it may relieve them that are widows indeed." It is just another way of saying, "There will be plenty of people needing the help of their brethren and sisters in Christ, and therefore let those who should care for any who are in such needy circumstances take charge of these distressed ones and not put a needless burden on the church of God." This was God's order in the early church, and it is still His order today. It is the business of the church to consider the poor and needy and minister to them as far as it can. On the other hand, it is but right that the members of a family provide for the needs of those related to them, if they can do so, and relieve the church of this additional load.

As children of God we are never to be selfish or stingy in ministering to those who are in poverty and distress. But we are not to encourage laziness, nor should the church be held accountable to support those whose own children can assume their care.

CHAPTER 12

Light on Life's Duties

1 Timothy 5:17–25

> Let the elders that rule well be counted worthy of double honour, especially they who labour in the word and doctrine. For the scripture saith, Thou shalt not muzzle the ox that treadeth out the corn. And, The labourer is worthy of his reward. Against an elder receive not an accusation, but before two or three witnesses. Them that sin rebuke before all, that others also may fear. I charge thee before God, and the Lord Jesus Christ, and the elect angels, that thou observe these things without preferring one before another, doing nothing by partiality. Lay hands suddenly on no man, neither be partaker of other men's sins: keep thyself pure. Drink no longer water, but use a little wine for thy stomach's sake and thine often infirmities. Some men's sins are open beforehand, going before to judgment; and some men they follow after. Likewise also the good works of some are manifest beforehand; and they that are otherwise cannot be hid. (vv. 17–25)

Continuing his exhortations to Timothy, Paul speaks again of elders, and here dwells on the respect due them. Those who are qualified to lead the people of God in this way and who have the responsibility of shepherding the flock of Christ should never be treated rudely or looked upon with contempt.

Those who manifest particular administrative ability are to be counted worthy of double honor, or as the marginal note puts it, of "double reverence."

While we see no scriptural authority for giving the title of "reverend" to a minister of the gospel, as is commonly done in Christendom, yet it is evident that this particular Scripture may have seemed to some to give sufficient authorization for the custom. For if the elders, who ruled well, are to be counted worthy of double reverence, then those not so distinguished are still to be revered. But it is worthy to note that, in our English Bibles at least, it is only God Himself to whom the title "reverend" is applied. In Psalm 111:9 we read, "Holy and reverend is his name." The Hebrew word so rendered is found many times in the Old Testament, however, and is often translated "dreadful," or "terrible."

Charles H. Spurgeon, who himself repudiated any such title, though a worthy minister of Christ, declared that if one sought the origin of this practice he would have to go back to Roman Row in "Vanity Fair." He used to say ironically that if one minister should designate himself as the Reverend Mr. So-and-So, it would be just as correct for others to speak of themselves as the Dreadful or Terrible.

While recognizing all this, we need to remember that those whom God honors should be honored by us, and any leader who manifests true godliness in his life and is characterized by marked ability to administer the affairs of the church of God is worthy of reverence, "especially they who labour," Paul tells us, "in the word and doctrine." By so speaking he makes it clear that all elders were not necessarily preachers or teachers. Some were, but this was a special gift of God. In support of what he had just written Paul cites the Old Testament Scripture, "Thou shalt not muzzle the ox when he treadeth out the corn" (Deut. 25:4). This links with, "The labourer is worthy of his reward." When threshing was done by oxen it would have been cruel indeed to have refused the due portion of grain to the hard-working, patient animals who were thus employed. And so as God's servants give themselves to earnest labor on behalf of others, it is only right that such labor be recognized and they themselves respected and, where necessary, properly supported. This is a principle laid down elsewhere in the New Testament (Luke 10:7), and to which God's people may well take heed.

The next admonition has to do with charges of irregular behavior, or even of sinful actions in connection with one who is thus recognized as a servant of Christ. It is sad indeed when people thoughtlessly and often willfully spread evil stories about a servant of Christ without ever making any investigation and when others give heed to these without seeking corroboration. It is sadder still if anyone brings a charge of misconduct against an elder unless the charge is substantiated by other witnesses. Then, indeed, if the accusation is proven to be true, the office of the offender must not be allowed to shield him from blame. On the contrary, Paul writes, "Them that sin rebuke before all, that others also may fear." The greater one's responsibility, the more careful he needs to be as to his personal character and behavior. No elder, however able and gifted, should attempt to shield himself from blame simply because of his office. The very fact that he serves the church in such a capacity makes him all the more accountable to live for God before the people whom he endeavors to instruct in holy things, or whom he seeks to guide.

If assemblies of God everywhere would keep these admonitions in mind, they would be saved from a great deal of sorrow and dissension. Where God's servants are recognized as His representatives, and their ministry is properly valued and their advice followed, blessing will result for the whole church. Where a spirit of independence and insubordination prevails, and believers generally look with indifference or even contempt upon those appointed by God to have the rule over them, who must give account for their souls at the judgment seat of Christ, the results are likely to be most disastrous.

It seems difficult for many of us to keep from extremes. We are inclined to overvalue those who minister the Word of God and bear rule in the church, and to look upon them as though above all criticism. Or, where a spirit of individualism prevails, we are inclined to undervalue God's servants and treat them somewhat as Korah, Dathan, and Abiram sought to treat Moses and Aaron in the wilderness, when they said, "Ye take too much upon you, seeing all the congregation are holy, every one of them, and the LORD is among them" (Num. 16:3). They failed to recognize the fact that it is God Himself who appoints and qualifies leaders or shepherds over His flock. These should be given proper deference, not in the sense of looking upon them as a priestly class who come in between the people of God and their Lord, but rather as the expression of God's goodness in caring for and shepherding His people as they go through the wilderness of this world.

It is a very sad thing when parents set the example before their children of belittling God's servants by calling attention, perhaps, to mistakes in interpretation of the Word, or ridiculing certain characteristic habits on the platform or elsewhere. These things naturally lead the children to think less of those who are seeking to help them, and so make it harder to reach them with the Word. Children should be taught to look upon the elders and ministers of Christ as servants of God, whose great concern is their eternal blessing. If parents will collaborate in this instead of detracting from the usefulness of a servant of God, they will help him to accomplish more than he could otherwise.

Concerning receiving accusations against an elder without full proof, may I refer to a somewhat amusing incident that I ran across lately. In a certain church bulletin that came to my hand I read the following statement from the pastor of a little church.

He said, "I have learned that a story is being rather widely circulated that on a recent occasion I forbade my wife to attend the services of another church, which were of a highly emotional character. When she refused to obey me and attended without my permission, I went to that church and dragged her out by the hair of the head, and beat her so severely that she had to be sent to the hospital. I feel it necessary to make a statement in regard to this story. In the first place, I never forbade my wife to attend any services to which she might wish to go. I have left her at perfect liberty to do as she pleases in matters of this kind. In the second place, I did not drag her by the hair of the head from such a service, nor did I beat her when I brought her home. In the third place, she was not so badly hurt that she had to be sent to a hospital, and she is not in the hospital now. And in the fourth place, as some of you know perhaps, I have never been married, so I have no wife to whom any of these things could apply."

It is very easy to start a false story going, and by the time it has passed through the lips of several persons it can ruin the testimony of the most devoted man of God. Mr. Moody used to say that a lie gets halfway around the world before truth gets its boots on to pursue it.

In verse 21 the Apostle lays another important charge upon Timothy, which has a wide application at all times. "I charge thee before God, and the Lord Jesus Christ, and the elect angels, that thou observe these things without preferring one before another, doing nothing by partiality." The expression, "the elect angels," may cause some to wonder why these holy beings should be brought in here, but there are other Scripture passages that show that angels are learning the wisdom of God in us. They behold what is going on in the church on earth. Doubtless they rejoice when they see God's Word being honored, and His people walking before Him in unity and in holiness of life. So the Apostle links them here with God Himself and our Lord Jesus Christ, as he charges Timothy to observe the things concerning which he has admonished him. The charge is surely not for Timothy alone, but is for all who have to do with government in the house of God here on earth. Nothing should be done out of deference to some favored few or to win the approval of certain individuals, but all should be done faithfully for the blessing of the church as a whole.

The next admonition is of great importance, particularly in days such as these in which our lot is cast, when one finds so many men going about through the country professing to be servants of Christ, perhaps representing some particular organization in which they are endeavoring to interest others in order to raise funds for the support of their work. Men like these have no right to expect to be taken into the fellowship of God's people and given endorsement simply on their own recommendation. Only too often churches have been altogether too gullible in receiving such men without making the slightest inquiry to find out their true standing, or from whence they come. It turns out often that such men represent themselves only and the money they raise is but for their own comfort and enrichment.

So Paul lays down the definite injunction: "Lay hands suddenly on no man." It is far better to make inquiry before taking up with a stranger than to find out afterward that he was utterly unworthy of confidence. It is quite possible to become so entangled as to be actually responsible, in measure at least, for the failures of unfaithful workers and false teachers. So the Apostle adds, "Neither be partakers of other man's sins: keep thyself pure."

In writing to the elect lady in his Second Epistle, John says, "If there come any unto you, and bring not this doctrine, receive him not into your house, neither bid him God speed: for he that biddeth him God speed is partaker of his evil deeds" (vv. 10–11). If we remembered that God holds us responsible for assisting and sustaining those who are unfaithful to His truth and whose behavior and teachings are of a subversive character, it would make us more careful to heed these words.

Verse 23 is the favorite text of practically every old drunkard who knows anything of the Scriptures. I would not dare attempt to say how many times this passage has been quoted to me by inebriates seeking to justify their indulgences in alcoholic liquor. "Drink no longer water, but use a little wine for thy stomach's sake and thine often infirmities." It is certainly a great mistake to take advice such as this and apply it as though spoken to everyone under all circumstances. Evidently Timothy was suffering from digestive disturbances brought about, no doubt, by the intensely alkaline water found in some parts of the lands through which he traveled. The native wines of that time, which were quite different from the wines we have today, were calculated to correct this condition, at least to some extent. So Paul prescribed a little wine, which is a far different thing to convivial drinking of intoxicating liquor. This is a prescription authorizing the use of the wine as a medicine not as a beverage. If the circumstances be the same, it is perfectly right and proper to follow the prescription, but one should be careful not to use a passage like this as license for carelessness in the use of strong drink of any kind.

Proverbs 23:31–32 says, "Look not thou upon the wine when it is red, when it giveth his colour in the cup, when it moveth itself aright. At the last it biteth like a serpent, and stingeth like an adder." There can be no mistake here as to the teaching of the Word of God in regard to the use of wine as a beverage. Generally speaking, it would be better to consult a good Christian physician before acting on Paul's advice to Timothy, lest one aggravate his symptoms instead of alleviating them.

In the closing verses of this section we have something extremely solemn. We are told that, "Some men's sins are open beforehand, going before to judgment; and some men they follow after. Likewise also the good works of some are manifest beforehand; and they that are otherwise cannot be hid."

These words might seem to require very little comment, and yet it is well to press them home upon our own hearts and consciences. "Some men's sins are open beforehand, going before to judgment." That poor drunkard staggering down the street needs no one to proclaim him as a sinner. His behavior makes manifest his moral condition. His sins are open, going before to judgment. Anyone can recognize them. The licentious libertine soon bears in his body the evidence of his loose living. Men cannot indulge in pernicious habits without their very appearance advertising their guilt. Their evil behavior is manifested by every step taken; their sins are evidenced to all. And judgment falls, in measure at least, upon them even in this world, as we read in Romans 1:27, "Receiving in themselves that recompence of their error which was meet."

Others may be just as wicked and just as godless along other lines, but their sins are not of the character that affect their bodies to any great extent, and so they are able to cover them up. They often go through life hiding their wickedness under a pretense of piety, but the day will come when all their sins will be manifest. When they leave this world they will find that those sins have followed them to the judgment bar of God, and every transgression and disobedience will receive a just recompense of reward. "Be not deceived; God is not mocked: for whatsoever a man soweth, that shall he also reap. For he that soweth to his flesh shall of the flesh reap corruption; but he that soweth to the Spirit shall of the Spirit reap life everlasting" (Gal. 6:7–8).

We have the other side in verse 25: "The good works of some are manifest beforehand." There are those who have abundant opportunity to do good to others, and they take advantage of it and are lavish in their efforts to bless and help their fellows. It is impossible to hide such philanthropy, however modest the individuals themselves may be who thus delight in assisting the poor and needy. They are rich in good works, and what wealth this is! Who would not like to be rich in this sense! But there are other quiet, timid souls who long to be a blessing and help to their fellows, but who are not so circumstanced that they can do all they desire along these lines. Nevertheless, they live their quiet, humble lives in the fear of the Lord, seeking to do the will of God. When the day of manifestation comes and all believers stand at the judgment seat of Christ, everything will come out, and the Lord will reward everyone according to his own works. He will give His own estimate of all that has been done for Him. Those who were not always able to carry out the desires of their hearts will hear Him say in that day, as He said to David of old, "Thou didst well that it was in thine heart" (1 Kings 8:18).

What comfort this should be to any of God's beloved people who have felt themselves hampered all their lives because poverty and straitened circumstances kept them from doing much that it was in their hearts to accomplish for Christ! How blessed to know that He estimates everything aright, and in that day His "Well done, thou good and faithful servant: thou hast been faithful over a few things, I will make thee ruler over many things: enter thou into the joy of thy Lord," will be spoken to all who have sought to honor Him in this scene.

CHAPTER 13

Contentment Versus Covetousness

1 Timothy 6:1–10

Let as many servants as are under the yoke count their own masters worthy of all honour, that the name of God and his doctrine be not blasphemed. And they that have believing masters, let them not despise them, because they are brethren; but rather do them service, because they are faithful and beloved, partakers of the benefit. These things teach and exhort. If any man teach otherwise, and consent not to wholesome words, even the words of our Lord Jesus Christ, and to the doctrine which is according to godliness; he is proud, knowing nothing, but doting about questions and strifes of words, whereof cometh envy, strife, railings, evil surmisings, perverse disputings of men of corrupt minds, and destitute of the truth, supposing that gain is godliness: from such withdraw thyself. But godliness with contentment is great gain. For we brought nothing into this world, and it is certain we can carry nothing out. And having food and raiment let us be therewith content. But they that will be rich fall into temptation and a snare, and into many foolish and hurtful lusts, which drown men in destruction

> and perdition. For the love of money is the root of all evil: which while some coveted after, they have erred from the faith, and pierced themselves through with many sorrows. (vv. 1–10)

The outstanding verse of this section is the sixth: "But godliness with contentment is great gain." The Apostle is stressing the importance of contentment as opposed to that spirit of covetousness which so characterizes men of the world and is often found even among the children of God.

We need to remember that many of the early Christians were bondmen. Conditions of society that prevailed at that time were such that there were more slaves in the Roman Empire than there were free men. Even when the gospel began to be disseminated widely throughout the Empire we do not read of any movement on the part of Christian leaders seeking to overturn the institution of slavery, and that for a very good reason. Political circumstances and economic conditions were such in that ancient, pagan world that those in bondage as slaves to Christian masters were in a far better position than they could possibly have been if they had been freed and turned out to shift for themselves. But gradually throughout the centuries that followed as the nations received the gospel, the slaves were freed. Slavery was an accepted economic condition when Paul wrote to Timothy, and many of the early Christians were under bondage. So when the Apostle speaks of "servants" here, it is not hired servants as such that he has in mind, but "as many servants as are under the yoke."

He exhorts these slaves to contentment. One might say that they had very little with which to be contented, but Paul would have them able to say as he himself did, "I have learned, in whatsoever state I am, therewith to be content" (Phil. 4:11). He found that Christ was sufficient for all circumstances, and, thank God, it is just as true today! We live in a time of great restlessness. Consider the strife between capital and labor with which our own nation is confronted. We never would have to face anything like this if Christian principles prevailed between the employer and the employee. But the spirit dominant generally is that of every man for himself, each attempting to get all he can for himself and to give as little work as possible in return. Christian men and women should be careful to follow the spirit of the admonition given here, "Let as many servants as are under the yoke count their own masters worthy of all honour, that the name of God and his doctrine be not blasphemed."

A Christian employee should not be content to give less than honest work for the payment he receives, and he should look up to and respect those whom he serves. If it happens that he is working for a Christian, then he is not to take advantage of the fact that both are members of the body of Christ. They "that have believing masters, let them not despise them, because they are brethren." It is so easy to expect more than one has a right to demand because the one who employs him is a Christian. The fact that both are Christians is not to change the attitude of the employee into one of self-will and independence of spirit, but should rather lead each to be considerate of the other. The very fact that the employer is also a believer is one reason why the other should do his part faithfully and give the very best possible service for the money he is receiving, "because they are faithful and beloved, partakers of the benefit. These things teach and exhort."

Paul next draws attention to the fact that what he has just said is in full accord with the teaching of the Lord Jesus Christ, who Himself took the servant's place. He said, "I am among you as He that serveth" (Luke 22:27). He warned His disciples against all self-seeking. He said, "The kings of the Gentiles exercise lordship over them; and they that exercise authority upon them are called benefactors. But ye shall not be so: but he that is greatest among you, let him be as the younger; and he that is chief, as he that doth serve" (Luke 22:25–26). He also said that He "came not to be ministered unto, but to minister, and to give his life a ransom for many" (Matt. 20:28). When He found His disciples disputing among themselves as to who should be greatest He said, "Whosoever will be chief among you, let him be your servant" (Matt. 20:27). And so the Apostle says here, "If any man teach otherwise, and consent not to wholesome words, even the words of our Lord Jesus Christ, and to the doctrine which is according to godliness; he is proud, knowing nothing."

Where do we find the words of our Lord Jesus Christ? In the four Gospels. To me it is a shocking thing when Christian teachers seem to relegate to a former dispensation the practical instruction given by the Lord while He was on earth as though it had no weight for Christians today. What the Lord Jesus Christ taught when He was here in person ought to guide us in our behavior one toward another and in our attitude toward God. I have often heard it said that the Sermon on the Mount is not for Christians. Undoubtedly, it was given primarily to the remnant of Israel, God's earthly people. It is instruction for the Jewish disciples of Christ while waiting for the setting up of the kingdom. But on the other hand we should not overlook the fact that the Lord Jesus said that "every one that heareth these sayings of mine, and doeth them not, shall be likened unto a foolish man, which built his house upon the sand: and the rain descended, and the floods came, and the winds blew, and beat upon that house; and it fell: and great was the fall of it" (Matt. 7:26–27). But, "whosoever heareth these sayings of mine, and doeth them, I will liken him unto a wise man, which built his house upon a rock: and the rain descended, and the floods came, and the winds blew, and beat upon that house; and it fell not: for it was founded upon a rock" (Matt. 7:24–25). The *whosoever* here is just as universal as the *whosoever* in John 3:16. Our Lord was speaking to His people throughout all the years while waiting for His return from heaven.

If a man denies the words of the Lord Jesus Christ, "he is proud, knowing nothing, but doting about questions [sick about questions]." Have you ever met any of these people who were sick about questions? They take one or two little points and are always hammering away on them. No matter what text they start with when they attempt to preach they always come back to their favorite theme. They get their minds fixed on some peculiar views and cannot seem to consider anything else.

I remember an old man when I was a lad who would rise to speak at every opportunity. He had only one topic, and that was that Judas was not present at the Lord's Supper. No matter what the subject under discussion might be he would break in with: "Brethren, I want to show you that Judas was not present at the Lord's Supper." We got so tired of it that we dreaded to see or hear him. I do not believe that Judas was at the Lord's Supper, but I would hate to have no other topic except that about which to talk.

Notice this expression: "Doting [or sick] about questions." It is a great mistake to get one or two things in the mind and constantly dwell upon them. As a result of this there comes "envy, strife, railings, evil surmisings, perverse disputings [quarrellings] of men of corrupt minds, and destitute of the truth, supposing that gain is godliness: from such withdraw thyself."

If these malcontents can show that they have a number of adherents they are convinced that the Lord is with them: "From such," the Apostle says, "withdraw thyself."

"But godliness with contentment is great gain." We have already seen in going through this epistle that *godliness* is literally "godlikeness"—that is, *true piety.* Godliness is great gain. We have received blessings, temporal and spiritual, from God, and our hearts should be going out to Him in gratitude. We should not be characterized by a spirit of restlessness. It is this spirit that dominates men of the world. You have heard of the Quaker who wanted to teach a lesson to his neighbors. So he had a large sign put up on a vacant lot next to his house, and on the sign he had these words painted: "I will give the deed to this lot to anyone who is absolutely contented." Any applicant was directed to apply next door. There was a man living in that community who had great wealth, and he drove by, saw the sign, stopped, and said to himself, "My old Quaker friend wants to give away his lot to anyone who is absolutely contented. If there is anyone in the community that ought to be contented it is I. I have everything I could wish for." So he went to the Quaker's house and knocked on the door.

The Quaker came to the door, and the man said, "I see you want to give that lot to anyone who is contented."

"Yes," said the Quaker.

"I think I can say that I am absolutely contented," the man said. "I will be glad if you will make the deed out to me."

"Friend, if thee is contented, what does thee want with my lot?" the Quaker asked.

This spirit of covetousness is noticeable in men of the world. The Jewish Talmud says that man is born with his hands clenched, but he dies with his hands wide open. Coming into the world he is trying to grasp everything, but going out he has to give up everything.

"For we brought nothing into this world, and it is certain we can carry nothing out. And having food and raiment let us be therewith content. But they that will be rich [they that are characterized by covetousness, who are determined to be rich, who make that their one great object in life] fall into temptation and a snare, and into many foolish and hurtful lusts, which drown men in destruction and perdition. For the love of money is the root of all evil." It should read, "a root of all evil."

There are some men who do not love money and yet are the victims of many other evil passions. But what the Apostle is telling us here is that once the love of money finds lodgment in the heart of man every known evil may be grafted on to it.

Years ago when I was in California I was setting out a small orchard, and the nurseryman who sold me some fruit trees said to me, "You have a great many gophers. It is going to be hard to keep the ground clear of them. But," he said, "I'll give you some trees that are grafted on bitter peach roots. The gophers will not touch these."

So he brought the trees grafted onto the bitter peach roots. I had quite a little orchard: cherries, several kinds of plums, two or three kinds of apricots, several kinds of peaches, almonds, and so forth, but they were all grafted onto the bitter peach roots. As I saw them being planted I thought of this text, "The love of money is *a* root of all evil: which while some coveted after, they have erred from the faith, and pierced themselves through with many sorrows."

So let us thank God for the grace that He has given us through Jesus Christ our Lord and has put within our hearts the desire to glorify Him. "He that spared not his own Son, but delivered him up for us all, how shall he not with him also freely give us all things?" (Rom. 8:32). God gladly gives to the one who has already received His Son. Just as the love of money in the heart is a root of all evil, so when the love of Christ comes into the heart, everything good may be grafted onto that.

CHAPTER 14

The Life That Really Counts

1 Timothy 6:11–21

But thou, O man of God, flee these things; and follow after righteousness, godliness, faith, love, patience, meekness. Fight the good fight of faith, lay hold on eternal life, whereunto thou art also called, and hast professed a good profession before many witnesses. I give thee charge in the sight of God, who quickeneth all things, and before Christ Jesus, who before Pontius Pilate witnessed a good confession; that thou keep this commandment without spot, unrebukable, until the appearing of our Lord Jesus Christ: which in his times he shall show, who is the blessed and only Potentate, the King of kings, and Lord of lords; who only hath immortality, dwelling in the light which no man can approach unto; whom no man hath seen, nor can see: to whom be honour and power everlasting. Amen. Charge them that are rich in this world, that they be not highminded, nor trust in uncertain riches, but in the living God, who giveth us richly all things to enjoy; that they do good, that they be rich in good works, ready to distribute, willing to communicate; laying up in store for themselves a good foundation against the time to come, that they may lay hold on eternal life. O Timothy, keep that which is committed to thy trust, avoiding profane

> and vain babblings, and oppositions of science falsely so called: which some professing have erred concerning the faith. Grace be with thee. Amen. (vv. 11–21)

In this particular section we have three definite charges given to Timothy personally, and one which he is to pass on to others. But we may well take to ourselves the charges given to him as well as the less particular one. We read, "But thou, O man of God, flee these things." This naturally leads us to ask what things are referred to. So we have to go back in our thoughts to that verse where we were warned against ignoring the words of our Lord Jesus Christ as set forth in the four Gospels and where we were urged not to give way to perverse disputings, and the verses that follow in which we are warned above all else to avoid covetousness because the love of money is a root of every evil.

Paul says to Timothy, "O man of God, flee these things." This expression "man of God" is used on a number of occasions in both the Old and New Testaments, and it always seems to mean the man who stands for God in a day of declension. Some of the prophets of old are so designated. Timothy here is spoken of as "man of God." And I am sure that you and I who know and love the Lord long to merit that appellation, to be men and women who honor God in a day when so many ignore or rebel against Him.

The man of God is told to flee covetousness, selfishness, and perverse disputings. He is to "follow after righteousness," which has to do with our attitude toward our fellow men. It is a vain thing to profess to be justified before God and made the righteousness of God in Christ while acting unrighteously toward others. The Christian is to be characterized by righteousness in all his dealings. "Godliness" has to do with our attitude toward God. "Faith" is that confidence in God which enables us ever to count on Him. "Love"—that love which goes out first to the One who loved us and gave His Son to die for us and then to all for whom He died. "Patience"—that patience which enables one to endure as seeing Him who is invisible. Then "meekness," which is the very opposite of the pride, vanity, and self-satisfaction that are so common to the natural heart. Meekness is a plant of great rarity. Even in many who have a reputation for godliness and for expounding the Word there is very little evidence of meekness. May God give us to become increasingly like Him who said, "Take my yoke upon you, and learn of me; for I am meek and lowly in heart: and ye shall find rest unto your souls" (Matt. 11:29).

"Fight the good fight of faith." We are to be good soldiers. Timothy primarily, but all believers are called upon to fight the good fight of faith. It is interesting to note that in the next epistle when we come to the last chapter which was written by Paul in a prison cell while waiting for martyrdom, he says, "I have fought a good fight, I have finished my course, I have kept the faith" (2 Tim. 4:7). He did not ask others to do that which he himself had not done.

"Lay hold on eternal life." Does not every believer possess eternal life? Yes. The moment we put our trust in the Lord Jesus Christ we have eternal life. There are many Scripture passages to support this, but a few will suffice:

> Verily, verily, I say unto you, He that heareth my word, and believeth on him that sent me, hath everlasting life, and shall not come into condemnation; but is passed from death unto life. (John 5:24)

> And as Moses lifted up the serpent in the wilderness, even so must the Son of man be lifted up: that whosoever believeth in him should not perish, but have eternal life. (John 3:14–15)

> He that believeth on the Son hath everlasting life: and he that believeth not the Son shall not see life; but the wrath of God abideth on him. (John 3:36)

So eternal life is the present portion of all believers. What does the Apostle mean, then, when he says, "Lay hold on eternal life"? It is an exhortation to make it a practical thing as we go through this scene. It is quite possible to trust in Christ and thus to have eternal life in the soul, and yet to drop down to a low spiritual level where one is not living in the reality of eternal life. He exhorts everyone of us to enter into that life which is unworldly and heavenly in character. When in this scene, Christ Himself was the manifestation of eternal life. It is a poor thing to talk about having eternal life while living for the things of the world. "Lay hold on eternal life!" As I realize that my life is hid with Christ in God I will look very lightly upon the things of this world. Its pleasures will not attract me; its treasures will not possess my soul. I can go through this world as using without abusing the things God gives me. Knowing Him, who to know is life eternal, everything else is of little importance. Thus one may lay hold on eternal life.

"Whereunto thou art also called, and hast professed a good profession before many witnesses." That was a nice thing for the older preacher to say to the younger. Paul took Timothy with him when he was a mere lad and instructed him in the work of the gospel. As he looks back over the years of service he can say, "You have confessed [for in place of the word *professed* we should read *confessed*] a good confession before many witnesses." It was a nice thing to be able to say to a younger servant of Christ. May it be true of every one of us!

A very definite charge was committed to Timothy in verses 13–14. "I give thee charge in the sight of God, who quickeneth all things, and before Christ Jesus, who before Pontius Pilate witnessed a good confession; that thou keep this commandment without spot, unrebukable, until the appearing of our Lord Jesus Christ." This is a very solemn charge indeed, and it should come home to everyone of us. We are commanded to keep the truth of God: "That thou keep this commandment without spot, unrebukable, until the appearing of our Lord Jesus Christ." Our Savior Himself was a Confessor when here on earth, and we are called to follow Him in confessing His name.

Observe how the name of Pontius Pilate is brought in here. Have you ever noticed that Pontius Pilate is mentioned in the greatest of the Christian creeds, so that in thousands of churches all over this world every Lord's Day, and on many other occasions, the name of the governor of Judea, who condemned our Savior to death, is linked with our Lord's name? He had the power to free the Lord Jesus Christ, and he said, "I find no fault in this man" (Luke 23:4). But instead of freeing Him, Pilate turned Him over to the multitude to be crucified. So professing Christians recite the creed, "Jesus Christ crucified under Pontius Pilate." Pilate will face that for all eternity. Oh, my friends, see that your confession is real in regard to the Lord Jesus Christ, that thus your name will never be held up to eternal infamy because of your unfaithfulness.

Our blessed Lord made a good confession before Pontius Pilate. He did not hold back the truth even though He knew it meant the cross because He was going there for your salvation and for mine. We, too, are called upon to maintain a good confession. "That thou keep this commandment without spot, unrebukable, until the appearing of our Lord Jesus Christ." This will be the great climax for believers when everything will be manifested, and they will be rewarded according to the results of their faithfulness down here. There is no discharge in this war (Eccl. 8:8). We are enlisted for life, or until we meet our Lord when He returns in power and glory. Then each one will be rewarded according to the measure of his devotedness to Christ and subjection to His Word.

Notice what is said in connection with His second coming: "Which in his times he shall show, who is the blessed and only Potentate, the King of kings, and Lord of lords." That is a striking expression. He is going to be manifested in His own times—those times we believe are drawing very, very near. It seems to many of us as we read Scripture carefully and then notice what is going on in the church, in the world, and in connection with Israel, God's earthly people, that the times of the Gentiles are near the close, and these will be followed by "his times" when He Himself will be the blessed and only Potentate.

That word *blessed* might just as well be rendered *happy.* When the Lord reigns, the earth will see a happy Ruler. I do not think there is any happy potentate now. I am sure the kings of Europe and in other lands are far from happy, nor are presidents of republics in any more cheerful state. No, there are no happy potentates today. They are so hampered by conflicting principles and contesting political parties that they find themselves almost helpless to carry out the things which they believe are for the betterment of the nations. But when the Lord Jesus Christ reigns He will be a happy Potentate, because in Him the world will see One who not only has the desire to do good, but also the power to enforce His authority everywhere; He will rule the nations with the iron rod of righteousness. When He reigns there will be no one to dispute His Word, for He will be the only Potentate. All the kingdoms of this world will become the kingdom of God and of His Christ.

In the next verse we read that He "only hath immortality." That is, He is the source or fount of immortality. All others derive it from Him. He dwells "in the light which no man can approach unto," in the full blaze of Deity, for "God is light, and in him is no darkness at all" (1 John 1:5). No mortal eye can stand that light. Only they who are in Christ can abide in its presence in peace. "Honour and power everlasting" are His, and it is He who in grace has opened up to sinners the gates of life.

Immortality in Scripture is connected with the body. Our blessed Lord Jesus Christ had a body that was not subject to death. It was possible for Him to die only by divine authority. He said concerning His life, "No man taketh it from me, but I lay it down of myself. I have power to lay it down, and I have power to take it again. This commandment have I received of my Father" (John 10:18). And so in that body which came back from the dead at His own command, He sits at the right hand of the Father. He only has immortality, but at the coming of our Lord Jesus Christ all believers will be raised or changed and will be gathered together unto Himself. "Who only hath immortality, dwelling in the light which no man can approach unto; whom no man hath seen, nor can see." Deity is invisible to creatures.

Then we have the charge which Timothy was to lay upon those to whom he ministered, and which comes home very definitely to any today who are in such circumstances that these words really apply to them: "Charge them that are rich in this world, that they be not highminded, nor trust in uncertain riches, but in the living God, who giveth us richly all things to enjoy."

This is a message to all those to whom God has entrusted wealth. You have nothing you did not receive. You are not a superior people because you have a few more dollars than some others, or because you are able to buy a few more stocks and bonds. Everything you have is by the mercy of God. Do not forget that riches may be here today and gone tomorrow. During the great depression of 1929 I met people every day who were rich one day and poor the next. People went to bed in those days thinking they were well-off for the rest of their lives, but they woke up the next morning to find that the bottom had dropped out of the market, and they had lost everything.

Even if riches are gotten rightly they may be lost overnight, but if they are riches ill-gotten—well, Scripture says, "As the partridge sitteth on eggs, and hatcheth them not; so he that getteth riches, and not by right, shall leave them in the midst of his days, and at his end shall be a fool" (Jer. 17:11). So if I am addressing anybody today who is piling up riches obtained unrighteously, I would suggest that you straighten things up as soon as you can. Take the place of Zacchaeus when he said, "Behold, Lord, the half of my goods I give to the poor; and if I have taken any thing from any man by false accusation, I restore him fourfold" (Luke 19:8). We are told to "trust . . . in the living God, who giveth us richly all things to enjoy." It is wonderful how happy one can be with very little if he has the Lord. Like the dear old lady who, when someone came to see her in her little attic, was found sitting down to a lunch of an onion, a piece of bread, and a glass of water. The visitor started to commiserate, "Oh," she said, "I have all this and heaven too." We are immensely wealthy if we have Christ.

Observe Paul's advice to the rich: "That they do good, that they be rich in good works, ready to distribute, willing to communicate; laying up in store for themselves a good foundation against the time to come, that they may lay hold on eternal life." As we have it here, the expression "eternal life" is just the same as that in verse 12. That is, "Lay hold on eternal life," which we have already received. But in the Greek text a different word is used, and why the translators did not indicate this I do not know. But the exact rendering should be "that they may lay hold on that which is *really* life."

You see, the rich man imagines, when he enjoys all the pleasures that his wealth can give him that he is seeing life, that he is having a good time. As he passes his hours in pleasure, he says, "This is life!" The Apostle says that is not life at all; that is just death. If you want to see life, if you want to enjoy life at its very best, then use what God has committed to your trust for the blessing of others. If you really want to be happy, and you are sure you know the Lord, if you have come to Him and taken your place before Him as a lost, guilty sinner, and trusted Him as your Savior, if you have passed from death unto life, then I can tell you what to do, not on my own authority, but as it is given here in the Word of God: begin today and use what God has given you for the blessing of others. Try to think of people in need who could be benefited by what you have hoarded away. Ask God to guide you as to using your money to the good of others that you may be rich in good works.

If a man is rich only in stocks, bonds, and real estate, when he dies he will have to leave it all behind. But if he is rich in good works, when he dies he will take these with him—that is treasure laid up in heaven. Be ready to distribute when opportunity is given, to use of your means for furthering the work of the Lord, assisting the needy, helping the lepers, relieving the blind, and caring for the orphans. Be ready to give. Do not hold back or say, "Oh, well, I suppose I ought to do it." Be glad that God has enabled you to help, and be willing to give. If you use your money in that way you will be laying up in store a good foundation against the time to come, for this is real life.

It is a terrible thing to be in the grip of covetousness. If you are afraid that perhaps the love of money is getting a hold on your soul, start giving some of it away and see how you feel! If you feel really glad, then you are still safe, but if it almost breaks your heart, then it is time to get down on your knees and pray to be freed from this sin of covetousness! It is going to ruin you unless you are delivered from it.

In closing we have another charge to Timothy—and it is one for us all—against being taken up with false theories. Many of these are being promulgated today, and we need to be guarded against them. "O Timothy, keep that which is committed to thy trust, avoiding profane and vain babblings, and oppositions of science falsely so called." Science is knowledge arranged in an orderly way. It is not mere theory unsupported by facts. When people talk about the science of evolution, they misuse the word, for evolution is not a science because it is contrary to fact. When they talk of certain other sciences which deny the truth of the Bible, they are using the word in a wrong way. A hypothesis is one thing; science is another.

"Keep that which is committed to thy trust, avoiding profane and vain babblings, and oppositions of science falsely so called: which some professing have erred concerning the faith." These false theories turn people away from the simplicity of the gospel of Christ and leave them in error and confusion of mind. It was never more important to give heed to such admonitions than in this day when science is glorified and revelation is denied.

PART 2

2 TIMOTHY

CHAPTER 1

A Godly Heritage

2 Timothy 1:1–7

> Paul, an apostle of Jesus Christ by the will of God, according to the promise of life which is in Christ Jesus, to Timothy, my dearly beloved son: Grace, mercy, and peace, from God the Father and Christ Jesus our Lord. I thank God, whom I serve from my forefathers with pure conscience, that without ceasing I have remembrance of thee in my prayers night and day; greatly desiring to see thee, being mindful of thy tears, that I may be filled with joy; when I call to remembrance the unfeigned faith that is in thee, which dwelt first in thy grandmother Lois, and thy mother Eunice; and I am persuaded that in thee also. Wherefore I put thee in remembrance that thou stir up the gift of God, which is in thee by the putting on of my hands. For God hath not given us the spirit of fear; but of power, and of love, and of a sound mind. (vv. 1–7)

This Second Epistle to Timothy was written from a dungeon death cell. It is the last of Paul's letters, as 1 Thessalonians is the first, which God has preserved for the edification of the church. Paul, of course, may have written, and probably did write, a great many more letters than the fourteen (including Hebrews) that we have in the Word of God. But these are the only ones which the Spirit of God both inspired Paul to write, and also which He included in the canon of Scripture.

The circumstances in connection with the writing of this last letter are very interesting. We do not get much information from the Scriptures themselves, except what we glean from that which Paul tells us in these Epistles and in that to Titus. Much has come down to us, however, from some of the earliest Christian writers which enables us to piece things together, and so to know something of the actual conditions under which the letter was penned.

We learn from the book of Acts that Paul was sent to prison in Rome, charged with endeavoring to incite an insurrection against the Roman government. For two full years he remained a prisoner under guard in his own hired house until he appeared before Caesar, and then he was set free because the charges which the Jews had brought against him were not sustained. He was permitted to take up again his work of ministering the gospel of the Lord Jesus Christ. So far as we can learn from these early records, he then went on to Spain and preached there for a time. There is a legend—I think it is only a legend—to the effect that he crossed over to the British Isles and that he was the first to preach the gospel in Britain, but there is no proof of this which careful historians accept. From Spain he retraced his steps and went back to the region of Illyricum, along the eastern shores of the Adriatic Sea. He visited a number of churches where he had preached before, and went to Crete and other places not visited previously.

He was arrested again at a time when there was a great persecution against Christians. During the first imprisonment Christianity was looked upon as a sect of Judaism, which was a legalized religion. But shortly afterward the city of Rome was burned down, and by many this was attributed to Nero's own order. Finding that he was greatly blamed for such iniquity he attempted to turn the onus from himself by putting it upon the Christians. He issued an indictment demanding that all Christians should be sought out everywhere in the empire as enemies of Rome and put to death. It was during this persecution that Paul was arrested again, and taken back to Rome and confined in the Mamertine dungeon.

If you visit the city of Rome today you can see that dungeon. You can go down into it, and as you look around at those bare walls and gaze up at the ceiling, where there is just a little hole in the center from which food was dropped down to Paul and water passed through in some kind of vessel, you get an idea of the suffering that he must have endured. There is no window whatsoever through which to look to the outside world. A river passes underneath, and there is a cleft in the floor where you can look down and see the water running. It must have been cold and damp in there at all times of the year, particularly in the winter. As I stood there I had some little realization of what it must have meant for God's servants in early days to devote themselves to the ministry of the Word of God. Surely in comparison the lines have fallen unto us in pleasant places.

Just how long Paul remained in that dungeon we do not know. Nero died in the sixty-eighth year of our era. So sometime before that, possibly about A.D. 66 or 67, Paul was led out from his prison one day to the place of execution on the Ostian Road. There he laid down his gray head upon a great stone, and in a moment the executioner's axe had decapitated him. Paul was absent from the body and present with the Lord.

Some time during those months he wrote this letter—the last letter of his that has come down to us. There is always something tender about the last message from one whom we have learned to love. How we thank God for the apostle Paul's ministry. How delighted we would have been if we might have known him and heard his message delivered from his own lips. Here is his last word to his son in the faith.

As we read this epistle we shall find again and again that it is a triumphant message, though it came from a dungeon death cell. The great outstanding theme of the letter is the importance of faithfulness to Christ in a day of declension. First Epistles are, almost invariably, given to teaching; the Second Epistles are given more to prophecy. Now prophecy is not simply foretelling, but it is forth telling—stirring up the hearts and minds of God's people by proclaiming the ministry suited to the times. As we read this letter we hear not simply the voice of the teacher, as in the First Epistle, but we hear the voice of the prophet calling us to increased devotedness to Christ as the days become darker.

We have the salutation in the first two verses: "Paul, an apostle [that is, a *sent one,* an *official messenger]* of Jesus Christ by the will of God, according to the promise of life which is in Christ Jesus." In the letter to Titus, Paul uses a similar expression, but adds these words, "which was given before the ages began." What promise of life in Christ Jesus was given before the ages began? The probationary ages which began after the fall of man. The promise of life was given in connection with the curse put upon Satan when God said to him, "I will put enmity between thee and the woman, and between thy seed and her seed: it shall bruise thy head, and thou shalt bruise his heel" (Gen. 3:15).

After their sin was committed, Adam and Eve had no reason at all to expect to live. They had every reason to expect that they would be destroyed immediately, but instead of that, in infinite grace, God gave the promise of life in Christ Jesus. He said that the Seed of the woman who should yet be brought into the world "shall bruise thy head, and thou shalt bruise his heel." Adam immediately accepted this as a promise of life, and we read that he changed his wife's name. He called her "Eve."

You will notice she is never called Eve until after the Fall. We read that in the beginning "God created man in his own image, . . . male and female created he them"(Gen. 1:27), and He called their name "Adam." When the man first beheld the wife God had given him, he called her *Ishah* (lady) because she was taken out of *Ish* (man). But after God gave the promise of life in Christ, Adam called her "Eve," for *Eve* means "the mother of all living." So Christ came and through Him God offers life to the world. Paul had gone through many lands proclaiming this message of life for all who believe the gospel.

"To Timothy, my dearly beloved son: Grace, mercy, and peace, from God the Father and Christ Jesus our Lord." We have noticed in looking at the previous epistle that when the Apostle addresses a church he simply says, "grace and peace," when he addresses individuals it is "grace, *mercy,* and peace." It is so in 1 Timothy and in that to Titus. In the case of the letter to Philemon he does not insert the word *mercy,* because he is addressing not only Philemon but also "the church in thy house." The church, as such, does not need mercy, but individuals do because individuals fail and, therefore, are in need of constant mercy.

The introduction to the letter is found in verses 3–7. The great thing which this introduction emphasizes, it seems to me, is the blessing of a godly heritage. Now grace is not inherited. Every individual has to be born again, no matter how pious and devoted his parents may have been. But on the other hand, it is a great thing to have a godly heritage, to have parents who have known and loved the Lord Jesus Christ.

I have in my desk an old, old photograph. It is a photograph of my great-grandfather, just a farmer in Aberdeenshire, Scotland. The photograph is almost faded out with age, though I have tried to keep it covered from the light because I wanted to have it as long as I might live for this reason: I have been told many, many times by those who knew my great-grandfather (people who have long since gone home to heaven but used to know me, and whom I knew as a child) they told me how that great-grandfather of mine, at the close of every day, used to gather all his family—and it was a large family—and all his farmhands—and he had a large farm—about him and have family worship. He always prayed for the salvation and the blessing of his children and his children's children unto the third and fourth generations—and I come in there. As I look at the grizzled face of that old Scottish farmer I thank God for a godly heritage, and I thank Him for the way in which He has answered prayer.

Oh, young men and young women, never undervalue the piety of your dear father and mother. If they know Christ, thank God for it. Thank Him that you have Christian parents. Do not imagine you belong to a generation better instructed than they. You may know a little more about the sciences of today, but I fear few of us know nearly as much as many of our Christian parents knew of the things of God and eternity.

Now Paul himself was indebted to a godly heritage. "I thank God, whom I serve from my forefathers with pure conscience." His mind went back over the centuries, and he realized that he came from a line of godly people who loved the Lord and loved the truth of God. Even though, as Saul of Tarsus, he misunderstood and was zealous in his effort to destroy all who were followers of Jesus of Nazareth, doubtless his conversion was in answer to prayers which were made long before the time came when he was brought to know and love the Lord Jesus Christ.

"That without ceasing I have remembrance of thee in my prayers night and day." Paul valued Timothy because of his love for Christ, and he adds, "Greatly desiring to see thee, being mindful of thy tears, that I may be filled with joy." Evidently Timothy was very tenderhearted and affectionate and wept over sinners and over his own sins. Paul delighted to think of this because Timothy was his own convert and later his companion in the ministry.

He reminds Timothy of his early training. He says, "When I call to remembrance the unfeigned faith that is in thee." We know from another passage of Scripture that Timothy's father was a Greek, and perhaps he was not a believer at all (Acts 16:1), but Timothy's mother and grandmother were Jewesses. They were pious women who loved the Word of God and taught it to Timothy. We are told in this same letter that, "From a child thou hast known the holy scriptures, which are able to make thee wise unto salvation through faith which is in Christ Jesus" (3:15). Now when the Apostle says that, he does not mean that Timothy knew the New Testament, for it had not been written at that time. When he was growing up in that home yonder in Lystra or Derbe, there was no New Testament, but his mother Eunice and his grandmother Lois taught him the things of God out of the Old Testament. No doubt many times as a lad he sat at their feet as they read those marvelous Messianic Psalms and prophecies of the coming Redeemer. One can imagine him asking what this meant and what that meant as the Scriptures were explained to him. So when the day arrived that Paul came to that region preaching the gospel, Timothy listened to the message, and the Spirit of God created faith in his heart, for "Faith cometh by hearing, and hearing by the word of God" (Rom. 10:17). So Timothy was saved by faith in Christ Jesus.

I repeat what I said in the beginning, grace is not inherited. It is not necessarily true that because your parents are Christians you will be saved. But unless a spirit of rebellion is developed against the things of God, the children will follow on in the steps of godly parents and be led on in the ways of God. As Christian parents we have a right to expect that our children will be saved if we bring them up in the nurture and admonition of the Lord. But we need to be careful that we walk before them so that they may see in us just what a Christian ought to be.

"Which dwelt first in thy grandmother Lois, and thy mother Eunice; and I am persuaded that in thee also." The faith dwelt first in the grandmother, then was manifested in the mother, and finally in young Timothy who, when he heard the gospel, was ready to believe and confess Christ as his Savior.

Timothy was still out preaching the Word. Paul says, "Wherefore I put thee in remembrance that thou stir up the gift of God, which is in thee by the putting on of my hands." When Timothy was leaving Lystra to go out into the work of the Lord, the elder brethren met together—the Presbyters as they are called—and placed their hands in loving fellowship upon his head. Paul was with them. And they prayed that God would give Timothy some special blessing, and in answer to prayer there was a definite gift bestowed upon him. Notice again the words here: "Wherefore I put thee in remembrance that thou stir up the gift of God, which is in thee by the putting on of my hands." In response to Paul's prayer of consecration as this young man went forth to preach the gospel, God gave him a special gift in order that he might be more useful in Christian service.

Then Paul urges him not to become lax, not to become careless, but to stir up the gift of God thus given. He says, as it were, Do not forget your responsibility, and do not let anybody terrify you. Do not be afraid of others, no matter how great the persecution may be and how great the hatred. "For God hath not given us the spirit of fear; but of power, and of love, and of a sound mind." These are the indications that one is really controlled by the Holy Spirit of God. These things will be manifest in the life. There will be power over sin. There will be power as we go out to win others to Christ. There will be power as we preach the gospel. There will be love for all men, "Because the love of God is shed abroad in our hearts by the Holy Ghost which is given unto us" (Rom. 5:5). Then he speaks of a sound mind. The Spirit of God will not lead into fanaticism. I have heard a great many people talk about being filled with the Spirit who, as far as I could see, gave every evidence of an unsound mind. They were taken up with all kinds of queer, fantastical, emotional experiences. Where the Holy Spirit controls there will be a sound mind. The Spirit of God will guard our intellect so that we will serve God in a reasonable and intelligent way. In this Christ Himself is our example.

In closing may I stress again the blessing and responsibility of a godly heritage? If I am addressing any who are still out of Christ and yet have had a true Christian home, who have had the blessing of faithful parents whose prayers went up to God daily on your behalf, and who read the Word of God in that home, remember that a tremendous responsibility rests upon you. You can be sure that God will never overlook your indifference and your carelessness as to the privileges you have enjoyed as a boy or a girl raised in such an atmosphere. I plead with you, therefore, to determine early in life that you are going to belong to the Christ of your father, that your mother's Savior will be your Savior and your God, that the Bible they loved will be treasured by you, and that your life will answer to the prayers that they have offered on your behalf.

CHAPTER 2

NOT ASHAMED

2 Timothy 1:8–18

Be not thou therefore ashamed of the testimony of our Lord, nor of me his prisoner: but be thou partaker of the afflictions of the gospel according to the power of God; who hath saved us, and called us with an holy calling, not according to our works, but according to his own purpose and grace, which was given us in Christ Jesus before the world began, but is now made manifest by the appearing of our Saviour Jesus Christ, who hath abolished death, and hath brought life and immortality to light through the gospel: whereunto I am appointed a preacher, and an apostle, and a teacher of the Gentiles. For the which cause I also suffer these things: nevertheless I am not ashamed: for I know whom I have believed, and am persuaded that he is able to keep that which I have committed unto him against that day. Hold fast the form of sound words, which thou hast heard of me, in faith and love which is in Christ Jesus. That good thing which was committed unto thee keep by the Holy Ghost which dwelleth in us. This thou knowest, that all they which are in Asia be turned away from me; of whom are Phygellus and Hermogenes. The Lord give mercy unto the house of Onesiphorus; for he oft refreshed me, and was not ashamed of my chain: but, when he was in Rome, he sought me out very diligently, and found me.

The Lord grant unto him that he may find mercy of the Lord in that day: and in how many things he ministered unto me at Ephesus, thou knowest very well. (vv. 8–18)

There is so much in these verses that I was almost tempted to divide this portion into about three sections. But in one way they are all linked together, so I thought it best to consider them all at one time. They are connected by that expression "not ashamed." We have it three times in these verses: first, in the admonition of Paul to Timothy; second, Paul's own declaration; and third, in that which he testifies concerning his friend, Onesiphorus.

I wish we might fix our attention upon these words, "not ashamed." In Romans 1:16 we have that declaration of the Apostle, "I am not ashamed of the gospel of Christ: for it is the power of God unto salvation to every one that believeth; to the Jew first, and also to the Greek." Why should anybody be ashamed of the gospel? It answers every question concerning sin and its remedy that the mind of man can possibly raise. God has opened up His heart to men in the gospel. It is His message concerning His blessed Son and the salvation He has wrought out for all who believe.

It was because of his faithfulness in proclaiming the gospel that Paul was in prison. And now, writing to his younger friend, he said, "Be not thou therefore ashamed of the testimony of our Lord." It is as though he said, "Timothy, you have something of which you need never be ashamed as you go forth in Christ's name, telling how God has given His only begotten Son up to the death of the cross that all who put their trust in Him might be redeemed from sin's guilt and power." There are preachers who never seem to have anything to say about the blood of Jesus or the cross on which He died. But this is God's own message to a lost world, and we to whom it has been committed should never be ashamed of it.

The Apostle adds, "Nor of me his prisoner: but be thou partaker of the afflictions of the gospel according to the power of God." He says, "Do not be ashamed of me." There might have been those who would say to Timothy, "You are linked up with that fellow, Paul. I understand he came to a bad end and is now in prison." It would be easy for Timothy to say, "Oh, I knew him somewhat, but I was not intimate with him." But Paul said, "Do not be ashamed of me, but speak out boldly and let people know you stand for the same things for which I stand, because it is for this that I am in prison. It is for you to be partaker of the afflictions of the gospel according to the power of God."

It is a great privilege to partake of the blessings of the gospel, but God has ordained that we should not only have a part in these privileges, but that we should also be permitted to suffer for Christ's sake. This is the only world in which we can do that. Nobody suffers for Christ in heaven. It is down here only that we have this blessed opportunity. We should ever count it a privilege to bear shame for His name's sake when we think of what He has done for us.

In verse 9 he says, "Who hath saved us." Are you sure that you have been saved? There is a lot of uncertainty with many about this question. Some people think of salvation as a process going on all through life, and eventually, if they are faithful enough, they hope to be saved. But the Apostle says, "Who hath saved us."

In the epistle to the Ephesians he writes, "By grace are ye saved [literally, by grace have ye been saved] through faith; and that not of yourselves: it is the gift of God: not of works, lest any man should boast" (2:8–9).

There is no reason why any believer in the Lord Jesus Christ should be uncertain in regard to this question of salvation.

It may sound humble to sing as John Newton wrote one time when he had a fit of despondency,

> 'Tis a point I long to know,
> Oft it causes anxious thought;
> Do I love my Lord, or no?
> Am I His, or am I not?

But that is not the language of faith. The man who believes God can say, He "hath saved us, and called us with an holy calling, not according to our works." We do not purchase salvation by good behavior or by anything else we can do, but it is "according to his own purpose and grace, which was given us in Christ Jesus before the world began"—that is, before the ages began. Before sin came into the world, God had made all His plans for redemption. It was not an afterthought with God. It was all arranged. The Devil thought he was ahead of God when he caused man to sin, but God had already prepared for man's redemption, and that redemption "is now made manifest by the appearing of our Saviour Jesus Christ, who hath abolished death."

It is written in Hebrews 9:27, "And as it is appointed unto men once to die, but after this the judgment." That is what makes death so terrible for the unconverted man: he has to face God in judgment after he leaves this life. But the Lord Jesus Christ has "abolished death, and hath brought life and immortality to light through the gospel."

Elsewhere it is written, "That through death he might destroy him that had the power of death, that is, the devil; and deliver them who through fear of death were all their lifetime subject to bondage" (Heb. 2:14–15). In the Old Testament even believers had a fear of death. They did not know the blessedness of an accomplished redemption; and so many of them were left in a state of doubt and uncertainty as to what death might mean. They could not all say with Job, "For I know that my redeemer liveth, and that he shall stand at the latter day upon the earth: and though after my skin worms destroy this body, yet in my flesh shall I see God" (19:25–26). Many did not understand that. But now Jesus has gone down into death and has come up in triumph. He says, "I am he that liveth, and was dead; and, behold, I am alive for evermore, . . . and have the keys of hell and of death" (Rev. 1:18). Thus He delivers them "who through fear of death were all their lifetime subject to bondage" (Heb. 2:15).

I have often used an illustration of this, and it might not be out of place to repeat it in order to make this clear. Years ago when I was preaching out in the mountains of California the Lord gave me the joy of seeing many souls saved. After they were converted it was my desire to baptize them, and I have always been very old-fashioned in my idea of baptism. I take them right down under the water. Of course, some of you may sympathize with me in my ignorance, but that is all right, I return the compliment. I have baptized in lakes, in rivers, in ponds, and even in horse-troughs.

One time we had quite a group to baptize, both men and women. It was in the winter, and winter in California is a rainy time. It was in the region where the only water available was in the Sacramento River, which runs high in the winter and is very dark because of the silt brought down from the hills. I went out the day before and scouted around to find a place that seemed to be fit. There was room for a good audience to stand on the bank. I waded out into the river to make sure it was all right. On the next day we gathered together. It had been noised around that there was to be baptizing, and so there were hundreds of people gathering from all over the countryside. We preached the gospel. I saw those who were to be baptized looking at that dark river, and away down in their hearts I am sure everyone of them wished they were Presbyterians! I could tell they did not want to walk down into the water; they did not know what kind of experience it might involve.

While the people were singing the final hymn, I left the company, walked out into the water, and went on until I reached the place suitable for the baptizing. I felt around to see that there were no deep holes or dangerous rocks. I could see that those who were to be baptized were watching me. Finally, I went back to the shore, and when I put out my hand they came one after another. They were not afraid anymore. Why? Because I had gone down into the dark river and had come up safely.

Jesus went down into the dark waters of death and came up in triumph. And those who have trusted in Him do not dread death. They know death simply means going home to be forever with the Lord.

Now the Apostle says, "It is this that I was sent to preach, for which 'I am appointed . . . an apostle, and a teacher of the Gentiles. For the which cause I also suffer these things.'" He was in prison. He was enduring much hardship. He was suffering for His name's sake who gave Himself for lost mankind. And in order that he might carry that gospel to the world, he had given up all his earthly ambitions. He had given himself wholly to this one purpose of carrying the message from nation to nation, from people to people, from city to city. Now they had put him in jail, and this seemed to be the end of life, for in a little while he was going out to die for Jesus' sake. But he could say, "Nevertheless I am not ashamed: for I know whom I have believed, and am persuaded that he is able to keep that which I have committed unto him against that day." Paul gloried in the privilege of suffering for Christ. He was not ashamed of his message or of his Lord.

Observe Paul does not say, "I know *what* I have believed." He did know what he had believed. He had no doubts about that. But it is one thing to believe *what,* and quite another thing to believe *whom.* He says, "I know whom I have believed, and I am persuaded that he is able to keep that which I have committed unto him against that day."

Again and again the questions come to me, either by mail or from people whom I meet, "Do you believe in the perseverance of saints? Do you believe that if a man is once saved he is saved forever?" I generally say, "I certainly do not believe in the perseverance of saints as such. I know them too well, for I am one myself. But I believe with all my heart in the perseverance of the Lord Jesus, and I am persuaded that he is able to keep that which I have committed unto him against that day."

The Apostle had committed his soul to the Lord, and he knew that He would not let him down. That is why he is able to say elsewhere, "For I am persuaded, that neither death, nor life, nor angels, nor principalities, nor powers, nor things present, nor things to come, nor height, nor depth, nor any other creature, shall be able to separate us from the love of God, which is in Christ Jesus our Lord" (Rom. 8:38–39). Do you know anything which is neither included in things present nor things to come? Do you know anything that is not included in life or in death? Paul says that nothing in death, nothing in life, nothing present, nothing to come, shall be able to separate us from the love of God which is in Christ Jesus our Lord.

Again he says to Timothy, "Hold fast the form of sound words." In other words, he is saying, "Timothy, do not let anything go that you have received from God. Cleave to the truth, and then in that day when you have to give an account you will have the Lord's approval because of your faithfulness." On the other hand, he adds, "Which thou hast heard of me, in faith and love which is in Christ Jesus." You know it is an easy thing to become very disagreeable and contentious, even when one is endeavoring to be faithful to truth. The servant of God is called upon to contend for the faith. He is to maintain an attitude of faithfulness to Christ and love to the brethren. As we walk in love toward our brethren and stand firmly for the truth, we will commend to others that truth which we seek to proclaim with our lips.

At the time that Timothy went into the service of the Lord, he was commended to the Lord in a special way by a group of the elder brethren at Lystra, Paul joining with them, as we have noted already. In answer to their prayers, God gave Timothy some special gift to fit him for the work. So here in verse 14 Paul says to him, "That good thing which was committed unto thee keep by the Holy Ghost which dwelleth in us."

Paul had heard that many in Asia had turned away from the truth, the simplicity which is in Christ. Timothy was in Asia at this time where Paul had labored years before, and where many Christians had been led away from the truth by certain evil-disposed men who had gone in among them, teaching things contrary to the grace of God. Many of the saints were getting bewildered and carried away with these teachings. Some had even gone so far as to repudiate Paul's doctrine and refused to accept him as an apostle. We see that in the epistle to the Galatians. This was a great grief to him.

"This thou knowest, that all they which are in Asia be turned away from me; of whom are Phygellus and Hermogenes." Now do not misunderstand. Paul did not say they were no longer Christians, but he declared that they had turned away from him. These false teachers had come in and turned the saints away from the full gospel message that Paul had taught them, and they had repudiated him, no longer recognizing him as an apostle of Christ.

Next he mentions one who had come from Asia, who had been very faithful to him and very true. Paul speaks most tenderly concerning him. I do not know what had happened, whether he had been imprisoned or martyred for Christ's sake, but something had taken place which led him to write, "The Lord give mercy unto the house of Onesiphorus; for he oft refreshed me, and was not ashamed of my chain."

Evidently this man was what we would call today a traveling man. He moved about, possibly on business, or it may be that in the work of the Lord he went from place to place. In the course of his travels he came to Rome while Paul was a prisoner there. "But, when he was in Rome, he sought me out very diligently, and found me." It might not have been easy to find Paul in that great city, but Onesiphorus inquired of one and another until he found him.

Paul said, "[He] was not ashamed of my chain." He was not ashamed to stand by that prisoner in the dungeon and say, "He and I are friends. He and I stand for the same things. We serve the same Master."

I repeat, I do not know what had happened, but in the next verse Paul says, "The Lord grant unto him that he may find mercy of the Lord in that day: and in how many things he ministered unto me at Ephesus, thou knowest very well."

"Not ashamed!" Paul says to Timothy. "I do not want you to be ashamed. Do not be ashamed of the testimony of God; do not be ashamed of those who suffer for Christ's sake." Paul himself was not ashamed. Onesiphorus was not ashamed. He boldly identified himself with the prisoner of the Lord.

So I pass the word on to you who know and love the Lord. May we never be ashamed of His name.

CHAPTER 3

SERVICE AND REWARDS

2 Timothy 2:1–13

Thou therefore, my son, be strong in the grace that is in Christ Jesus. And the things that thou hast heard of me among many witnesses, the same commit thou to faithful men, who shall be able to teach others also. Thou therefore endure hardness, as a good soldier of Jesus Christ. No man that warreth entangleth himself with the affairs of this life; that he may please him who hath chosen him to be a soldier. And if a man also strive for masteries, yet is he not crowned, except he strive lawfully. The husbandman that laboureth must be first partaker of the fruits. Consider what I say; and the Lord give thee understanding in all things. Remember that Jesus Christ of the seed of David was raised from the dead according to my gospel: wherein I suffer trouble, as an evil doer, even unto bonds; but the word of God is not bound. Therefore I endure all things for the elect's sakes, that they may also obtain the salvation which is in Christ Jesus with eternal glory. It is a faithful saying: For if we be dead with him, we shall also live with him: if we suffer, we shall also reign with him: if we deny him, he also will deny us: if we believe not, yet he abideth faithful: he cannot deny himself. (vv. 1–13)

Many have noticed long since that in this second chapter the believer is presented in seven distinct aspects, and we shall eventually have opportunity, I trust, to look at each one of these. But in this section before us we see him in four aspects: a son in verse 1; a soldier in verse 3; an athlete in verse 5, and a husbandman in verse 6. As we go on through the chapter we find him presented as a workman in verse 15, a vessel to the glory of God in verse 21, and a servant of the Lord in verse 24. In all these different characters the believer is called upon to represent the Lord Jesus Christ in this scene.

In this first section the subject particularly dealt with is the question of service and rewards. "Thou therefore, my son, be strong in the grace that is in Christ Jesus." Paul speaks of Timothy as his son, because it was through his preaching that Timothy was brought to know the Lord. So Paul was pleased to think of Timothy as his own child in the faith.

Now every believer is a child of God. We are not children of God by natural birth. I know there is a teaching abroad that all men are God's children. All men are God's creatures. He is the Creator of them all. But only those who are born again are spoken of as children of God, and they alone are entitled to look up into the face of God and say, "Our Father."

I trust that we all know the reality of this; that everyone of us can look back to a time when, through infinite grace, we trusted the Lord Jesus Christ as our Savior and so began the walk of faith. "Be strong in the grace that is in Christ Jesus." Grace is God's favor bestowed upon those who have no merit of their own. We are saved by grace, stand in grace, and are to walk in grace.

In verse 2 the Apostle instructs Timothy to pass on to others the things that had become most precious to him. We may all take this to heart. "And the things that thou hast heard of me among many witnesses, the same commit thou to faithful men, who shall be able to teach others also." Paul had instructed Timothy as to the great historic facts of Christianity and the doctrines based upon them. These had been attested by many witnesses. It became the responsibility of the younger preacher to make these things known to others, that the truth might be spread far and wide. This is the true apostolic succession, as distinguished from a sacerdotal system such as Rome and some others advocate.

All down through the history of the church this is the way God's truth has been made known. One generation receives the truth, is led to believe in the Lord Jesus, that generation passes the Word of truth on to the next generation, and so it has been through the centuries. And upon us rests this same responsibility. That which we have received is not for ourselves alone. As God has opened up precious truths in His Holy Word, it is not simply for our own enjoyment. But our responsibility is to pass on to others that which means so much to us, to bring others into the same blessed fellowship of the truth of God. This will often take a great deal of self-denial. The path of witnessing for Christ may be a very hard one. God has never promised His children an easy time in the world. Our Lord Himself said, "If any man will come after me, let him deny himself, and take up his cross daily, and follow me. For whosoever will save his life shall lose it: but whosoever will lose his life for my sake, the same shall save it" (Luke 9:23–24).

So Timothy is commanded in verse 3 to "endure hardness, as a good soldier of Jesus Christ." Each Christian is called to do valiant soldier service, contending earnestly for the faith once for all delivered to the saints (Jude 3). This figure is frequently used in the Epistles. Note especially 2 Corinthians 10:3–5; Ephesians 6:10–18; 1 Thessalonians 5:8, as well as here. The Christian life is a constant warfare. We have three subtle and cruel enemies ever arrayed against us—the world, the flesh, and the Devil—and against all these we are called to make a resolute stand. We do not fight in our own strength, but as we are empowered by Him whose soldiers we are.

So we find Paul, with zeal unquenched, urging upon the younger preacher, Timothy, that he persist relentlessly in the battle for righteousness against all the hosts of evil. He, himself, maintains this soldier character to the last, as he realized that his fighting days were nearly ended and that soon he should give account of his part in this warfare, when he would stand at the judgment seat of Christ to receive the crown of righteousness, the divine recognition of faithful service, as he looked on to the appearing of his great General who had fought and overcome on his behalf so long before.

The figure of the soldier suggests obedience to orders, rigid discipline, holding the body in subjection, and valor in defense of the truth. These things should characterize all Christ's servants. The path of devotion to Christ is not an easy way. It calls for steadfast endurance and abiding faith. These are soldier qualities every Christian needs in order that he may overcome in the warfare with iniquity.

Then again a true soldier must be separated from the affairs of this world. "No man that warreth entangleth himself with the affairs of this life; that he may please him who hath chosen him to be a soldier." He has to leave many things to which he has been accustomed. So you and I who were poor, godless worldlings have now been separated to the Lord and are called to walk apart from the world in devotion to the great Captain of our salvation.

In verse 5 the believer is looked upon as an athlete, as a man striving for mastery: "And if a man also strive for masteries, yet is he not crowned, except he strive lawfully." A more accurate or literal rendering is, "If a man contend in the games, yet is he not crowned if he have not observed the rules." One would gather as he reads these Epistles that Paul in his youth must have had a keen interest in athletics, for he gives so many illustrations from the athletic games, such as racing and wrestling contests. He applies these to the life of a Christian.

It is a well-known principle in athletics that a man who enters a contest will not receive the reward unless he observes the rules of the game. Many years ago when I was laboring among the Laguna Indians in the southwest, I went into a store one Saturday night and found my Indian interpreter standing on a chair reading from a newspaper. The store was filled with Indians, and he was translating what he read into their language. The newspaper contained an account of the Olympic games that had been celebrated that year in Stockholm, Sweden. The man who had won most of the prizes was a full-blooded Indian, known as Jimmy Thorpe. How thrilled these Indians were as my interpreter was reading and telling all about his victories. He told them how at the time when the gold medals and other trophies were being conferred, the King of Sweden himself decorated Jiminy Thorpe, and taking him by the hand before all the people, he said, "You are to be congratulated. You are the greatest amateur athlete in the world today." Those Indians were most enthusiastic as they heard that one of their own people had won out over so many other athletes.

I went into that same store some weeks afterward. Again the place was filled with Indians, and my interpreter was reading to them. But the result was not the same. There were no bright, happy faces. I wondered what had made the change. I learned that some white men in this country had been so indignant that an Indian had carried off so many prizes that they had been searching into the Indian's past. They found out that one summer while attending Carlyle School in Pennsylvania he had served on a baseball team for $5.00 a week. That information was sent to the committee, who referred it to the King of Sweden. The result was that the king had to write Jimmy Thorpe to send back all the medals and trophies because he was not entitled to them. The athletic games, the king said, were for amateurs and not for professionals. Jimmy had taken money for playing ball and so was a professional. Poor Jimmy sent a letter to the King of Sweden, saying, "I am only a poor, ignorant Indian, and I did not know that the fact I had accepted $5.00 a week one summer for playing on a baseball team had made me a professional. I didn't mean to deceive." He sent back all his honors.

As these Indians listened to this account, they were stirred deeply. They could not understand the white man's way. But no athlete is entitled to reward if he has not observed the rules.

As Christians we are here wrestling with the powers of evil, and we are to be rewarded only if we observe the rules. The rules are contained in the Word of God. We must conform our behavior to the Word if we are to be rewarded.

In verse 6 the believer is referred to as a farmer. *Husbandman* is the old-fashioned English word for a tiller of the soil. First we read, "The husbandman that laboreth must be first partaker of the fruits." More literally, we might read, "The farmer that laboureth first becomes partaker of the fruits." The farmer has his work to do: his plowing, sowing, harrowing, and reaping before he can enjoy his fruit. We are here to labor. Oh, what a day it will be when at last we come before our Lord at the judgment seat of Christ and become partakers of the fruit! How much it will mean to any of us who have had the privilege of winning souls for Christ, to stand at that judgment seat with those whom we have brought to Him, and say, "Behold I and the children whom Thou hast given me!" How sweet His "Well done" will sound to these ears of ours in that day of reward!

Paul adds, "Consider what I say; and the Lord give thee understanding in all things." If we are going to labor faithfully for Christ, we must have Christ before us.

"Remember that Jesus Christ of the seed of David was raised from the dead according to my gospel." *"Remember . . . Jesus Christ."* It is really a battle cry—as of late we often hear the slogan, "Remember Bataan." The word *that* is omitted from the Revised Version. When pressed by the foe, even to the point where one despairs of life, let us remember Him who could not be overcome by death but arose in triumph from the grave. It is He who beckons us on to ultimate victory. His promises never fail of fulfillment. Jesus Christ went down into death, bore the judgment our sins deserved in order that we might be saved, and then came up in triumph from death as the Captain of our salvation. And for His sake, says the Apostle, "I suffer trouble, as an evil doer, even unto bonds; but the word of God is not bound."

As we have seen previously, Paul wrote this letter in a Roman dungeon. Though he was imprisoned as a malefactor, he had a conscience void of offense toward God and man because he was there for the gospel's sake. He said, "I endure all things for the elect's sakes, that they may also obtain the salvation which is in Christ Jesus with eternal glory." The elect are those who receive Christ, those who put their trust in Him, who rest their souls for eternity upon Jesus Christ who died for sinners.

The last three verses of this section are considered by scholars generally as a little poem or hymn, probably sung in the early Christian assemblies. It is written in metrical form, and therefore might have been so used.

> It is a faithful saying: For if we be dead with him, we shall also live with him: if we suffer, we shall also reign with him: if we deny him, he also will deny us: if we believe not, yet he abideth faithful: he cannot deny himself. (vv. 11–13)

What words are these, "We have died with him!" Those of us who have taken Him as Savior are seen by God as identified with Him in His death. We have a right to say, as Paul said, "I am crucified with Christ: nevertheless I live; yet not I, but Christ liveth in me: and the life which I now live in the flesh I live by the faith of the Son of God, who loved me, and gave himself for me" (Gal. 2:20). We died with Him, so we also live with Him. And if we suffer with Him, we shall share His glory. We shall reign with Him when He comes again. All believers suffer *with* Him, but all do not suffer for Him to the same extent.

On the other hand, if we who have professed to be Christians turn away from Him and deny His name and prove our unreality, then He will deny us. He said, "Whosoever shall confess me before men, him shall the Son of man also confess before the angels of God: but he that denieth me before men shall be denied before the angels of God" (Luke 12:8–9). "Whosoever therefore shall be ashamed of me and of my words in this adulterous and sinful generation; of him also shall the Son of man be ashamed, when he cometh in the glory of his Father with the holy angels" (Mark 8:38).

It is a challenge to reality. Mere profession does not save. We need to receive Christ and trust Him with all the heart, and then we shall boldly confess His name. If we believe not, yet He remains true. He can never go back on His word. Our unbelief cannot change His plan or purpose, nor alter His truth—He cannot deny Himself. He must be faithful to His own character.

Unless we distinguish carefully between salvation by pure grace and service or discipleship, for which a sure reward is promised, we are likely to become confused when considering such a portion as this. We are not called to fight our way to heaven. But as already bound for that blessed country, we are called to be soldiers in our Lord's army, contending against every unholy thing that would impede our progress or bring dishonor upon our Savior's name. For all such service we shall be rewarded "in that day," that is, when we stand at the judgment seat of Christ (2 Cor. 5:10).

Our conflict in this age of grace is not, as Israel's was in the past, with adversaries of flesh and blood. We do not draw the sword to destroy the opponents of our Lord and His gospel. But we fight with the sword of the Spirit against spiritual powers of evil—the unholy forces that would, if they could, nullify our testimony by leading us into things that bring dishonor upon the name of Him whose we are and whom we serve (Acts 27:23).

CHAPTER 4

Rightly Dividing the Word of Truth

2 Timothy 2:14–18

> Of these things put them in remembrance, charging them before the Lord that they strive not about words to no profit, but to the subverting of the hearers. Study to show thyself approved unto God, a workman that needeth not to be ashamed, rightly dividing the word of truth. But shun profane and vain babblings: for they will increase unto more ungodliness. And their word will eat as doth a canker: of whom is Hymenaeus and Philetus; who concerning the truth have erred, saying that the resurrection is past already; and overthrow the faith of some. (vv. 14–18)

We noticed that in this second chapter the believer is presented in seven distinct aspects. We have considered him already as a son, a soldier, an athlete, and a farmer. Now we come to consider him as a workman or an artisan, a laborer in this scene to the glory of God.

Referring to what he has already brought to our attention, the Apostle says in verse 14, "Of these things put them in remembrance." That is, of the importance of being wholeheartedly out for God as a soldier; of the necessity of remembering that an athlete contending in the games does not receive the victor's reward unless he observes the rules, and, therefore, of the importance of going by the Word of God, for this is our Book of rules.

If we are to be partakers of the fruit, there must be labor first. Even as a farmer must plow, sow, and cultivate the ground before he can expect a crop, so if we are to receive a reward at the judgment seat of Christ we must labor faithfully and devotedly now.

Then we do not want to forget that our Lord Jesus Christ died for us and has been raised again by the power of God. We do not want to forget that this message of the gospel is ours to proclaim to lost ones, no matter what is entailed in that, no matter whether there be suffering or imprisonment. For Paul it did mean imprisonment and death. But we are to remember, "It is a faithful saying: For if we be dead with him, we shall also live with him: if we suffer, we shall also reign with him: if we deny him, he also will deny us." All these things are to be kept in remembrance as we go on in the service of the Lord.

Then notice this special command, "Charging them before the Lord that they strive not about words to no profit, but to the subverting of the hearers." It is so easy to become occupied with minor details in regard to the Christian message, which, after all, have nothing to do with the great fundamental issues. How many there are who become occupied with some of these side issues, stressing them on every occasion, and even dividing the people of God because of them, instead of placing the emphasis on the great central truths of the Word that are so tremendously important. We are not really serving the Lord when we are striving with one another about things that are unprofitable. We are called to contend for the faith, not to become contentious. As a rule, it is these minor things that lead to contention when they are emphasized out of all proportion to their relative importance.

On the other hand, the Christian needs to give himself to a careful study of the Scriptures in order that he may understand the truth and use it aright, as we get it in verse 15: "Study to show thyself approved unto God, a workman that needeth not to be ashamed, rightly dividing the word of truth." Paul himself says elsewhere that he was not at all concerned about having man's approval. In writing to the Corinthians he says, "With me it is a small thing that I should be judged of you, or of man's judgment" (1 Cor. 4:3). It made little difference to him whether men approved or blamed, but he was greatly concerned to have the approval of the Lord. And this is what he stresses here for us—that we need to study the Word so that we may be pleasing to Him who called us by His grace, who, has saved us in His infinite, loving-kindness, and has left us in this scene that we may glorify Him.

In the Old Testament we read of Abraham's first son—that son, Ishmael, who was born of Hagar. You remember that all that was contrary to the mind of God. Abraham began to wonder if God was going to fulfill His promise in regard to Isaac who was to be born of Sarah. Instead of blessing coming to the household, there was trouble. Instead of Ishmael being a joy to Abraham and to Sarah, he was the very opposite. We read of Ishmael that he "shall dwell in the presence of all his brethren" (Gen. 16:12). Then long years afterward the time came for him to leave this life, and we are told, "He died in the presence of all his brethren" (Gen. 25:18). Ishmael was a man, as far as we have any record, who was never, in all his life, in the presence of God but lived in the presence of his brethren. He was one whom the world would admire. He was a man of the great open spaces, a daring warrior and a great hunter. He had all the characteristics that men like to see in one another, and so he had the approval of his brethren. But he did not have the approval of God.

It is quite possible for a man, even in the work of the Lord, to be approved by his brethren and not have the approval of God. And so the importance of heeding these words, "Study to show thyself approved unto God." For not he who commends himself, nor whom his brethren commend is necessarily thus approved, but he whom the Lord commends. He whom God approves is the man who makes much of this blessed Book, who studies it and seeks to live in the power of the truth herein revealed. David prayed, "Order my steps in thy word" (Ps. 119:133). God has given us His Word, not only that it should unfold wonderful and precious things to us concerning the great, eternal future, but that through it we may learn how God would have us live as we go through this scene.

The Lord Jesus prayed for His disciples, "Sanctify them through thy truth: thy word is truth" (John 17:17). As we meditate on the Word and let it direct our lives, we will be sanctified in this practical sense. Oh, the neglected Bibles in the homes of the people of God! Wherever you find a neglected Bible you will also find a fruitless life. You will find a life out of fellowship with God. There will be nothing in that life that really honors Him. But where you find that the Word of Christ dwells richly in the heart and mind of a believer, then God will be glorified. So we are to study to show ourselves approved unto God.

Studying the Bible means more than just reading it casually. It means giving it our careful attention, comparing one Scripture with another, weighing the words in every chapter and every verse. But even as we read the verses and meditate upon them, we should avail ourselves of every possible help that might open things up to us more clearly, making it the business of our lives to become more familiar with the Holy Scriptures. "Study to show thyself approved unto

God, a workman that needeth not to be ashamed, rightly dividing the word of truth." We are to avoid slipshod work or carelessness in our consideration of the Word. We are not to put our own ideas in the place of the Word. If you were building a house and hired a man to do the work for you, you would hand him the blueprints and instruct him to go by them. Suppose he were to go ahead and work according to his own desires and his own ideas. You would soon discharge him. He might attempt to argue with you and to insist that his ways were better than yours, but you would say, "This is not what I wanted."

"I know it isn't according to the blueprint," he might reply,; "but I thought it would be very much nicer this way."

You would say, "But I do not care what you thought. I engaged you to build this house according to the plans I gave you."

So it is when we are working for the Lord. Many of us are very, very busy in what we call Christian service, but we are not working in accordance with the Word. And someday we will stand ashamed before God because of the wasted years that we have spent following our own ideas instead of being guided by His instruction. But if we are to be thus guided we must know the Word and be able to use it aright: "A workman that needeth not to be ashamed, rightly dividing the word of truth." Other translators have suggested different renderings for "rightly dividing the word of truth." J. N. Darby's version reads, "Cutting in a straight line the word of truth." That, I think, is very suggestive. You see, the Bible does not deal with one great subject only, neither does it speak to just one class of people. So as we study the Word, it is always important to ask, as we read, For whom was this written? What did God have in mind in giving it? Is it for me? Is it about me, or does it have to do with some other group of His people?

In 1 Corinthians we find three definite groups brought before us to whom God has spoken in His Word: the Jews, the Gentiles, and the church of God (1 Cor. 10:32). To rightly divide the word of truth we need to consider what parts of the Word are written particularly to God's earthly people, the Jews—what parts have to do with the Gentile nations as such, and what parts are particularly intended for the guidance and direction of the church. There are these three classes of people in the world today

There was a time when there were only two. Before Pentecost there were two classes—Jews and Gentiles. Since Pentecost, since the Holy Spirit descended, we have three groups in the world. The third group is known as the church of God. And this blessed Book has a great deal in it that is addressed particularly to the church of God. Now all Scripture is *for* me, but all Scripture is not *about* me. The Old Testament Scripture is for me just as truly as the New Testament, but

I will look in vain for guidance as to my path through this world, for instance, in the book of Leviticus or in the book of Chronicles and some other Old Testament books. Yet all are part of God's Word, and are profitable, "For whatsoever things were written aforetime were written for our learning, that we through patience and comfort of the scriptures might have hope" (Rom. 15:4). But we have to learn to rightly divide the Word and see to whom God was speaking and why. Then we will be able to see what is for our instruction as we seek to do what He commands.

These distinctions are not the only ones to be considered when we attempt to rightly divide the Word of truth. There are many other lines of truth. For instance, there is that which has to do with our salvation, which is by the grace of God and to which no works of ours can be added. But it would be a great mistake if we neglected a kindred line of truth which has to do with our responsibility as children of God in this world. On the other hand, we have Scripture passages that deal with our justification, which depends entirely upon the finished work of the Lord Jesus. I cannot be saved by works of righteousness which I have done. Yet there are other Scripture passages that lay tremendous stress upon good works which should follow faith in Christ, and they show me that only as we engage in good works can we expect reward at the judgment seat of Christ.

Before He went away Jesus said He was going to send the Comforter, the Holy Spirit, who would operate in a different way from which He had ever done before. The Savior said, "He dwelleth with you, and shall be in you" (John 14:17). The Holy Spirit was with the people of God before the flood. We read, "Enoch walked with God: and he was not; for God took him" (Gen. 5:24). Noah was a preacher of righteousness for 120 years while he was building the ark. The Spirit of Christ was preaching in him, as Peter tells us in 1 Peter 3:20. And God said, "My Spirit shall not always strive with man" (Gen. 6:3). It was the Spirit after the flood that guided the patriarchs and directed them. It was the Spirit of the Lord in a pillar of cloud by day and a pillar of fire by night that led Israel through the wilderness. It was He who spoke in the prophets. And when Jesus was here on earth we read that the Spirit was given to Him without measure.

Thus He was with the apostles. They had wonderful privileges such as no other children of God ever had—the presence of the Spirit was with them in the Person of the Christ of God Himself, "for God giveth not the Spirit by measure unto him" (John 3:34). Jesus said, "He dwelleth with you," and then looking forward to the new dispensation, He added, "and [He] shall be in you" (John 14:17). This is the great truth in our present age. If you are born of God, if you are a Christian, then the Holy Spirit dwells in you. What a wonderful thing it is to know that the Spirit of God is moving about through this world in you and in me. This divine Person is dwelling in us! "Know ye not," says the Apostle, "that ye are the temple of God, and that the Spirit of God dwelleth in you?" (1 Cor. 3:16).

Oh, how careful we ought to be then as to our behavior when we realize that the Spirit of God, this heavenly Guest, dwells in our very bodies—those of us who have trusted the Lord Jesus as our Savior. We need to cut in straight lines the Word of truth regarding the Person and work of the Holy Spirit.

We also need to learn how to distinguish between salvation by grace and reward for service. We cannot lose our salvation, but we are ever in grave danger of losing the reward that the Lord will give to all those who are faithful to Him.

There are many other lines of truth that we ought to understand clearly in order to be workmen that need not to be ashamed, cutting in straight lines the Word of truth.

"But shun profane and vain babblings: for they will increase unto more ungodliness." This word *babblings* means "baby talk." Men may have great learning who are just given to babblings in spiritual matters. Take the great philosophers. What is a philosopher? A man who is trying to find out the mystery of the universe. And here is a Book that will tell him all about it, but he turns his back on that which God has revealed and tries to find things out for himself. "Professing themselves to be wise, they became fools" (Rom. 1:22). The mature Christian is instructed out of the Word of God. He is not misled by these babblings. People say sometimes, "I don't think it makes any difference what a man believes if he is only sincere." But you know down in your heart that this is not true.

You might drink poison, sincerely believing that it is pure water, but it would kill just the same as if you knew its nature and took it with intent to commit suicide. No, you do not believe it makes no difference what one believes so long as he is sincere. You know in your own heart that one can be sincerely wrong and bring disaster upon himself and others. What we need to be sure of is that God has spoken in His Word. It is only the Word that will keep us right. When we turn from the Word to human theories, which are just profane and vain babblings, they will increase unto more ungodliness. Experience proves that no man's life will be in the right who refuses the truth of the Word.

We must know the truth of God in order to walk in the truth. The Apostle here instances two men who failed in this—two men who went off into error and misled others. He says, "And their word will eat as doth a canker: of whom is Hymenaeus and Philetus; who concerning the truth have erred, saying that the resurrection is past already; and overthrow the faith of some."

"And their word will eat as doth a canker"—like a cancerous growth in the body, it will get worse. Here are two men who had evidently been fellow laborers to some extent with the apostle Paul. At any rate, they had been recognized as Christian preachers and teachers, but they drifted from the truth. They turned away from God's revealed Word and took up with vain speculation, saying, "The resurrection is past already." And with this false teaching they overthrew the faith of some. It might seem a small thing as to whether the resurrection has passed or not, but it is a tremendous thing. If they were right, then our hope in Christ would go for nothing.

God grant that you and I who profess subjection to Christ may give increased attention to this Book so that our Bibles may not be neglected but read faithfully in dependence upon the Sprit of God, as He opens up the truth to us that we may walk in the power of it.

CHAPTER 5

Separation and Service

2 Timothy 2:19–26

> Nevertheless the foundation of God standeth sure, having this seal, The Lord knoweth them that are his. And, let every one that nameth the name of Christ depart from iniquity. But in a great house there are not only vessels of gold and of silver, but also of wood and of earth; and some to honour, and some to dishonour. If a man therefore purge himself from these, he shall be a vessel unto honour, sanctified, and meet for the master's use, and prepared unto every good work. Flee also youthful lusts: but follow righteousness, faith, charity, peace, with them that call on the Lord out of a pure heart. But foolish and unlearned questions avoid, knowing that they do gender strifes. And the servant of the Lord must not strive; but be gentle unto all men, apt to teach, patient, in meekness instructing those that oppose themselves; if God peradventure will give them repentance to the acknowledging of the truth; and that they may recover themselves out of the snare of the devil, who are taken captive by him at his will. (vv. 19–26)

In our consideration of the earlier verses of this chapter we have seen the believer presented in five different aspects: as son, soldier, athlete, husbandman (or farmer), and workman or artisan. And now in these closing verses we come to consider him in two more characters: first, as a vessel for the display of the glory of God; and, second, as the servant of the Lord.

All that we have here is in view of declension and corruption coming into the professing church. It had begun already and, as we have seen, Hymenaeus and Philetus were misleading many. There is something rather interesting about their very names, which suggest that these men were of agreeable and pleasant character, and yet they were using their natural charm to mislead God's people. *Hymenaeus* is really the "singing" man; the word means "a wedding song." *Philetus* is the "kissing" man; the name means "a lover." The two would make quite a combination! These two false teachers were seeking to mislead the churches.

You can never be sure about a man just because he has a nice, attractive personality. Satan's ministers, like Satan himself, can appear in very persuasive roles. And so the Apostle tells us to be on our guard. No matter how much false teaching may come in, "Nevertheless the foundation of God standeth sure." Our blessed Lord said to Peter, "Upon this rock [Christ the Son of the living God] I will build my church; and the gates of hell shall not prevail against it" (Matt. 16:18). All the power of the enemy has been brought against the church of God down through the centuries, but the church abides and will abide until the Lord comes again. "Having this seal, The Lord knoweth them that are his." We may not know for certain, but it is not for us to judge.

We are responsible, though, to walk in the truth and depart from error. "And, let every one that nameth the name of Christ [or, of the Lord] depart from iniquity." Separation from known evil is mandatory. We are commanded to depart from iniquity, or lawlessness, to depart from self-will, and this includes all forms of ungodliness and worldliness. "Let every one that nameth the name of Christ depart from [lawlessness]," depart from having his own way. This will settle many questions for young Christians. So many young Christians say, "Is it wrong to do this? Is it wrong to do that?" That is hardly the question for you as a Christian to ask. Rather, one should inquire, "Is this something that is profitable? Is it something that will help to make my Lord more precious to me? Will it draw me closer to Him?" Every Christian should have the desire to please the Lord Jesus Christ. True Christian living is subjection to His will.

In the next verse the Apostle uses a little parable. He says, "In a great house [that is, a house of a wealthy person, a mansion] there are not only vessels of gold and of silver, but also of wood and of earth; and some to honour, and some to dishonour." As you enter such a great house you may see on the sideboard in the dining room beautiful silver, golden, or cut-glass goblets, and other vessels, while out in the kitchen and in the cellar there will be earthenware vessels and vessels of baser metal. "Some to honour, and some to dishonour." The vessels unto honor are for the pleasure of the family and are used for the refreshment of their guests. These vessels are displayed openly where all may see them. They must be kept clean and bright, and after each using they must be separated from the other vessels of less value.

"If a man therefore purge himself from these, he shall be a vessel unto honour." Every Christian should be a vessel for the display of God's glory in this scene—a vessel unto honor. But in order that this might be, we need to be clean, not only clean ourselves but also clean as to our associations. We are to purge ourselves by separating from evil associates and from everything unholy in our lives. Thus we shall be vessels "unto honour, sanctified, and meet for the Master's use, and prepared unto every good work."

Let me try to illustrate this. Suppose we are in a great house. The host has brought some friends home, and he desires to refresh them. So he goes into the dining room and looks for some beautiful goblets, but there are none. He calls a servant and asks where the goblets are—the silver goblets, or the cut glass, whatsoever they may be. The servant replies, "Why, there was a banquet here last night, and all the vessels are out in the kitchen to be cleaned." The host directs him to go out and clean them and bring them to him so that his guests may be served. The servant has to separate these valuable vessels from all the mixture that is out there in the kitchen sink. Every piece has to be purged, individually cleansed, and so made fit for use. Then he brings them in and presents them to the host, who takes the vessels and uses them unto honor.

You see, Christians are like those vessels. There is a sad mixed condition in Christendom today, saved and unsaved, often united in the same church fellowship. There are those who profess to know the Lord and those who have never confessed Him, and people wonder why there is so little power and blessing. If you want to please the Lord who has made you His own, you must separate yourself from all that is unclean. Then you will be "a vessel unto honour, sanctified, and meet for the master's use, and prepared unto every good work."

Paul adds, "Flee also youthful lusts." Youth is the time when natural desires predominate, when carnality and concupiscence are very manifest. We are to flee these things. We are not to allow them to have dominion over us. On the contrary, we are to "follow righteousness, faith, [love], peace, with them that call on the Lord out of a pure heart." We are to be separated from those who are unclean, and to fellowship with those who walk before God in righteousness and holiness of life.

In the next place we are warned against occupation with trivial matters. He says, "But foolish and unlearned questions avoid, knowing that they do gender strifes." After we have taken our stand for God, after we come out from the world or from some worldly church where the truth is no longer preached, it is so easy to be self-satisfied and occupied with minor questions, and thus lose the sweetness and attractiveness that should characterize one who is separated to the Lord Himself.

In the next verse we have the seventh aspect in which the believer is presented in this chapter. "And the servant of the Lord must not strive; but be gentle unto all men, apt to teach, patient." It is difficult sometimes to be faithful to the truth without becoming quarrelsome. We are called upon to "earnestly contend for the faith which was once delivered unto the saints" (Jude 3). We are not to be contentious or querulous, manifesting a bad spirit about right things, but we are to be characterized by the spirit of grace even as we stand firmly for the Word of God. "In meekness instructing those that oppose themselves." The man who opposes the truth is working harm to himself. We need to remember this. It will make us kind and considerate as we seek to recover them from error, "if God peradventure will give them repentance to the acknowledging of the truth." Some who were the bitterest enemies of the gospel have been won for Christ by faithful dealing. "And that they may recover themselves out of the snare of the devil, who are taken captive by him at his will."

This second chapter of 2 Timothy has a very important message for us in these times of declension, when corruption and false doctrines abound on every hand. It is a time when believers in the Lord Jesus Christ need to be more careful about their contact with things that defile the Spirit. We need to take to heart these words, and separate ourselves from everything unclean and everything unholy. We need to yield ourselves entirely to the Lord to be guided and directed by Him that we may be vessels unto honor. Let us so manifest Christ in our lives that we will make the truth attractive to those who do not know Him. Sometimes we do harm to the very cause for which we stand because of the harsh and unkind spirit that dominates us. It took a long time for many of us to see some of these things, and, therefore, we should be patient and sympathetic in dealing with others who have not yet understood them.

In writing to the Philippians, the Apostle says, "Let us therefore, as many as be perfect, be thus minded: and if in any thing ye be otherwise minded, God shall reveal even this unto you. Nevertheless, whereto we have already attained, let us walk by the same rule, let us mind the same thing" (3:15–16).

CHAPTER 6

Characteristics of the Last Days

2 Timothy 3:1–9

In his First Epistle to Timothy, as we have seen, Paul speaks of the latter times, and he depicts conditions that have long since been fulfilled—conditions, however, which were still far in the future when he wrote. He said, "In the latter times some shall depart from the faith, giving heed to seducing spirits, and doctrines of devils; speaking lies in hypocrisy; having their conscience seared with a hot iron; forbidding to marry, and commanding to abstain from meats, which God hath created to be received with thanksgiving of them which believe and know the truth."

We have only to look back into what we speak of as "the Dark Ages" to recognize the fulfillment of these words. We have it in the Romish apostasy, in looking upon an unmarried nun or a celibate monk as a holier person than the Christian wife and mother, or husband and father. "Commanding to abstain from meats," as though these were conducive to lead one into sin, and the abstinence from them had a tendency to make one holier. We know how all that has been fulfilled.

And now we come farther along the stream of time. We come to our own times—the last days of this Second Epistle. (In order to give a somewhat fuller exposition of this passage than time permitted in the oral address, I have substituted a portion of my book, *The Midnight Cry.*) Paul says:

> This know also, that in the last days perilous times shall come. For men shall be self-lovers, money-lovers, boasters, proud, blasphemers, disobedient to parents, unthankful, unholy, without natural affection, unforgiving, false accusers, incontinent, savage, haters of good, traitors, heady, high-minded, lovers of pleasures rather than lovers of God; having a form of godliness, but denying the power thereof; from such turn away. For of this sort are they who creep into houses, and lead captive silly women laden with sins, led away with manifold desires, ever learning and never able to come to the knowledge of the truth. Now as Jannes and Jambres withstood Moses, so do these also resist the truth: men of corrupt minds, reprobate concerning the faith. But they shall proceed no further: for their folly shall be manifest unto all, as theirs also was. (vv. 1–9, 1911 VERSION)

These are the great outstanding features of the "last days"—closing the church dispensation and to be immediately followed by the coming of the Lord. Can any believer in Holy Writ doubt our being now in the very midst of them?

But it may be here objected: "When have men in general been other than as here depicted? Is not this but a repetition of what Paul has already said in describing the heathen world in his day (Rom. 1:29–32)? In what special sense are they any more characteristic now than then?" To these very natural queries I reply that such things, indeed, ever described the heathen, but in 2 Timothy 3 the Holy Spirit is describing conditions in the *professing* church in the last days! It is not the openly wicked and godless who are being depicted here. It is those who have a form of godliness while denying its power. This is what makes the passage so intensely solemn and gives it such tremendous weight in the present day. There are twenty-one outstanding features in this prophecy of church conditions in the last days, and that each may have its due weight with my reader I touch briefly on them in order.

1. "Men shall be self-lovers." It is men self-occupied, as contrasted with the godly of all ages who found their joy and delight in looking away from self to God as seen in Christ. This is the age of the egotist in matters spiritual as well as carnal. They find their God "within" them, we are told, and not without. They make no secret of it. When they profess to love God, it is themselves they love.

2. "Money-lovers." Is it necessary to speak of this? Colossal fortunes heaped together by men who profess to believe the Bible and its testimony! What a spectacle for angels and demons! There was one Simon Magus of old. He has myriads of successors in the professing church today, and the command "not to eat" with a covetous man or an extortioner is in most places a dead letter indeed.
3. "Boasters." Read the so-called Christian papers, attend Christendom's great conventions of young people or old. Listen to the great pulpiteers of the day. What is their theme? "Rich, and increased with goods, and have need of nothing!" Great swelling words are rapturously applauded by people dwelling in a fool's paradise, even when uttered by men who are tearing the Bible to shreds, and who deny practically every truth that it contains.
4. "Proud." So proud as to glory in their shame—congratulating themselves on the very things the Word of God so unsparingly condemns. Proud of their fancied superiority; proud of their eloquence; proud of their miscalled "culture"; proud of their very impiety, which is hailed as the evidence of broad-mindedness, and a cultivated intellect! How nauseating it must all be to Him who said, "Take my yoke upon you, and learn of me; for I am meek and lowly in heart."
5. "Blasphemers!" Yes, there it is—that big, ugly word that one hesitates to use, but which is chosen by the Holy Spirit Himself to describe the men drawing salaries as ministers of Christ who use their office to impiously deny His name! Blasphemers! Aye, the whole host of the new theologians, miscalled "higher critics," and all their ilk—all who deny the Deity of the Son, His virgin birth, His holy humanity—blasphemers, every one, and as such to be judged unsparingly in the harvest of wrath so near at hand! And think of the disloyalty to Christ of Christians—real Christians, I mean—who can sit and listen to such men week after week and are too timid to protest, or too indifferent to obey the Word, "From such turn away!"
6. "Disobedient to parents." It is one of the crowning sins of the age, and indicates the soon breaking-up of the whole social fabric as at present constituted. Opposition to authority is undoubtedly one of the characteristic features of the time. Children will not brook restraint, and parents have largely lost the sense of their responsibility toward the rising generation. Does this seem unduly pessimistic? Nevertheless, a little thoughtful consideration will, I am sure, convince any reasonable person of its truth. And it may be laid down as an axiom, that children not

trained in obedience to parents will not readily be obedient to God. We have been sowing the wind in this respect for years, as nations and as families. The reaping of the whirlwind is certain to follow.

7. "Unthankful." It is the denial of divine Providence—utterly forgetting the Source of all blessings, both temporal and spiritual. Straws indicate the turn of the wind, and even "so small a matter," as some may call it, as the giving-up of the good old-fashioned and eminently scriptural custom of thanksgiving at the table, we may see how prevalent is the sin of unthankfulness among professed Christians. Go into the restaurants or other eating houses. How often can you tell the believer from the unbeliever?
8. "Unholy." The godly separation from the world according to the Bible is sneered at as "bigotry" and "Puritanism." In its place has come a jolly, rollicking worldliness that ill comports with the Christian profession. Piety—that characteristic Christian virtue—how little seen now! It is not necessary to be outwardly vile to be unholy. Giving up the line of separation between the believer and the unbeliever is unholiness.
9. "Without natural affection." The foundations of family life are being destroyed. Unscriptural divorces and all their kindred evils cast their dark shadows over the professing church, as well as over the body politic.

   On the next unholy octave I need not dwell particularly. To enumerate them is enough to stir the heart and appall the soul when it is remembered how they are tolerated and spreading through the great professing body.

10. "Unforgiving"
11. "False accusers" (Let us beware lest we be found almost unwittingly in this satanic company!)
12. "Incontinent"
13. "Savage"
14. "Haters of good"
15. "Traitors"
16. "Heady"
17. "High-minded"

   This last accounts largely for the daring things proudly uttered by learned doctors against Scripture and the great fundamentals of the faith, and complacently accepted by unregenerate hearers. Surely, the time has come "when they will not bear sound teaching, but according to their own desire shall heap to themselves teachers, having itching ears" (2 Tim. 4:3, 1911 VERSION).

18. "Lovers of pleasure rather than lovers of God." Would you not almost think the words were written by some fiery-souled exhorter of the present day? How aptly they characterize in one brief clause the greatest outstanding feature of the religious world. The church of God has gone into the entertainment business! People must be amused, and as the church needs the people's money, the church must, perforce, supply the demand and meet the craving! How else are godless hypocrites to be held together? How otherwise can the throngs of unconverted youths and maidens be attracted to the "services"? So the picture show and the entertainment, in the form of *musicale* (sacred, perhaps!) and minstrel show, take the place of the gospel address and the solemn worship of God. And thus Christless souls are lulled to sleep and made to feel "religious" while gratifying every carnal desire under the sanction of the sham called the church! And the end? What an awakening!
19. "Having a form of godliness, but denying the power thereof." Men must have some form of religious expression, and so the outward thing is sustained after the life is gone out of it. Thus formality prevails where regeneration, conversion to God, the Spirit's sanctification, and everything really vital has long since been virtually denied. The bulk of so-called "church-members" do not even profess to have been saved or to be Spirit-indwelt. All this is foreign to their mode of thought or speech. The gospel, which alone is "the power of God unto salvation," is seldom preached and, by the mass, never missed! Could declension and apostasy go much further? Yet there are still lower depths to be sounded!
20. Feminism. No, you will not find the word—but read verse 6 again, slowly and thoughtfully. Does it not indicate a great feminist movement in these dark days? "Silly women, laden with manifold desires"—craving what God in His infinite wisdom has forbidden them: authority, publicity, masculinity, and what not? Thus they leave their own estate and make a new religion to suit themselves. Is it a matter of no import that just such emotional women were the tools used by Satan for the starting and propagating of so many modern fads? Need one mention Mesdames Blavatsky, Besant, and Tingley of Theosophy; the Fox sisters' relation to modern Spiritism; Mrs. Mary Baker Glover Eddy and her host of female practitioners in the woman's religion miscalled "Christian Science"; the neurotic Ellen G. White and her visionary system of "Seventh-day Adventism"; Ella Wheeler Wilcox and her associates in the spreading of what they have been pleased to denominate the "New Thought," which is only the Devil's old lie, "Ye shall be as gods," in a modern garb; and the women-expounders

of the "Silent Unity," or "Home of Truth" delusions? All these are outside the "orthodox" fold. But when we look within, what a large place has the modern feminist movement secured in the affections of women who profess to believe the Bible, but who unblushingly denounce Paul as "an old bachelor" with narrow, contracted ideas, little realizing that they are thereby rejecting the testimony of the Holy Spirit. It is one of the signs of the times, and clearly shows toward what the professing body is so rapidly drifting!

21. "Ever learning, and never able to come to the knowledge of the truth"—and that by their own confession. They are "truth-seekers." Ask them if it be not so. They confess it without a blush and consider it humility thus to speak. According to these apostates, the church which began as "the pillar and ground of the truth" is, in this twentieth century of its existence, "seeking" the truth, thereby acknowledging they never yet have found it! Truth-seekers! Yet the Lord Jesus said, "I am the way, the *truth,* and the life" (John 14:6). Why then seek further? Because they have drifted away from Him and His Word, so they go on, ever learning, ever seeking, and ever missing the glorious revelation of the *truth* as it is in Jesus.

Well, this is the end. Declension can go no further than to deny the Lord that bought them, until He Himself shall remove His own to the Father's house. Then the apostate body remaining will declare, "We have found the truth at last!" and they will worship the Antichrist, believing the Devil's lie and calling it the truth. And how comes such delusion? "And for this cause God shall send them strong delusion, that they should believe the lie; that they all might be judged *who believed not the truth* but had pleasure in unrighteousness" (2 Thess. 2:11–12, emphasis added, 1911 VERSION).

As for those who have been the leaders in turning others from the truth, what will happen to them? "Now as Jannes and Jambres withstood Moses, so do these also resist the truth: men of corrupt minds, reprobate concerning the faith. But they shall proceed no further: for their folly shall be manifest unto all men, as theirs also was." That is, in due time God is going to deal in judgment with those who mislead the ignorant and unwary, and who turn them unto fables which encourage them to live in sin and follow after the lusts of the flesh.

This is God's picture of the last days. And I challenge you to look about you and see if these are not the conditions that characterize a great part of Christendom today—no reality, no power, yet much profession. God give us to be genuine, to be real, that eternal things may so grip our souls that we will live and do the work and be real witnesses for Him.

CHAPTER 7

The Authority of the Holy Scriptures

2 Timothy 3:10–17

> But thou hast fully known my doctrine, manner of life, purpose, faith, longsuffering, charity, patience, persecutions, afflictions, which came unto me at Antioch, at Iconium, at Lystra; what persecutions I endured: but out of them all the Lord delivered me. Yea, and all that will live godly in Christ Jesus shall suffer persecution. But evil men and seducers shall wax worse and worse, deceiving, and being deceived. But continue thou in the things which thou hast learned and hast been assured of, knowing of whom thou hast learned them; and that from a child thou hast known the holy scriptures, which are able to make thee wise unto salvation through faith which is in Christ Jesus. All scripture is given by inspiration of God, and is profitable for doctrine, for reproof, for correction, for instruction in righteousness: that the man of God may be perfect, throughly furnished unto all good works. (vv. 10–17)

In contrast to the false teaching and evil practices of many in the last days, we now have the example of Paul himself set forth under nine heads, after which he stresses the importance of cleaving to the Holy Scripture as our security against error.

First we read, "But thou hast fully known my doctrine." Paul was preeminently a teacher. He was also an evangelist, but his great gift was that of teaching, unfolding the truth that God had revealed to him for the blessing of others.

Second, inasmuch as Timothy had been associated with Paul for a number of years—ever since the early days when he first began to witness for Christ—the Apostle writes to him, "Thou hast fully known my . . . manner of life." It is a pitiable thing when one's behavior is not in accordance with his doctrine. You have heard of the preacher who preached, "Do as I say, but not as I do." That is a poor testimony. We cannot lift men higher than ourselves. If one is not living for God, is not walking with Christ, then he cannot be a real blessing to other people.

In writing to the Thessalonians, Paul said, long years before he wrote 2 Timothy, "Our gospel came not unto you in word only, but also in power, and in the Holy Ghost, and in much assurance; as ye know what manner of men we were among you for your sake. And ye became followers of us, and of the Lord, having received the word in much affliction, with joy of the Holy Ghost" (1 Thess. 1:5–6). Paul and his companions lived such lives that they gave power to their message.

Third, we read, "Thou hast fully known my . . . purpose." It is most important that we have a purpose and stand by it when that purpose is not to magnify oneself but rather in all things that Christ might be magnified.

Fourth, "Thou hast fully known my . . . faith"—not the faith that saves but that faith which enables one to lay hold upon God day by day and triumph over all circumstances.

Fifth: "Longsuffering"—enduring all things for Christ's name's sake and the gospel. Coupled with that is "charity," the sixth in order. This word has come to mean "almsgiving," but that is only a very small part of its meaning. The original word translated "charity" is not simply almsgiving, though that may be included, but it is unselfish love and compassion for men everywhere, thus enabling one to rise above jealousy, envy, covetousness, and every unholy tendency. We are to love even our enemies, no matter how they treat us.

Seventh: "Thou hast fully known my . . . patience." It takes a lot of patience to go on in the work of the Lord. So many things try and exercise one's heart. But if we recognize the fact that "all things work together for good to them that love God, to them who are the called according to his purpose" (Rom. 8:28), we can patiently endure even the most distressing experiences.

Eighth and ninth, the Apostle adds, "Persecutions, afflictions," which he had to suffer for Christ's sake. Timothy knew a great deal about them. He knew what Paul had gone through at the beginning in Antioch, in Iconium, in Derbe, and in Lystra, where Timothy lived as a lad. It was at Lystra that Paul, having performed a great miracle, had difficulty to keep the people from worshiping him and Barnabas, his companion, as gods. Later these same people were stirred up by unbelieving Jews and tried to kill Paul. They thought they had done so and dragged his body outside the city gate, leaving it there as refuse. However, as the disciples gathered about him in great distress and were about to make arrangements to bury him, he opened his eyes and indicated there was no need of a funeral for the present.

Timothy was familiar with all these things, but Paul could say, "Out of them all the Lord delivered me."

You and I sometimes think we suffer if people cross our wishes, if they find fault with our motives. But I am sure it could be said of most of us, as Paul said to the Hebrew Christians, "Ye have not resisted unto blood, striving against sin" (Heb. 12:4). Many Christians in other lands have been called upon to suffer excruciatingly, to suffer in ways we have never known. Unto us it is given not only to believe on Him but also to suffer for His sake.

"Yea, and all that will live godly in Christ Jesus shall suffer persecution." If to some extent we are not the objects of the world's hatred, if we do not have the disapproval of those who despise Christianity, if we are not evil spoken of as were the prophets of God of old, then we may very well raise the question as to whether we are living godly lives or not. Persecution is inevitable for those who are faithful to God in a world like this, where "evil men and seducers shall wax worse and worse, deceiving, and being deceived." The world is ripening for judgment. It goes on and on in rebellion against God and His Christ, and its doom cannot be delayed much longer.

I know some people have the idea that the whole world is to be converted and all men brought to the knowledge of our Lord Jesus Christ by the preaching of the gospel. But Scripture gives no hint of anything of the kind. In fact, we find it teaches the very opposite. Our Lord said, "As the days of Noah were, so shall also the coming of the Son of man be" (Matt. 24:37). The world was not converted in the days of Noah. The mass of men were given over to violence and corruption. And the Lord Jesus Christ put the question, "When the Son of man cometh, shall he find faith on the earth?" (Luke 18:8). The nearer we get to the end, the higher is the rising tide of rebellion against God.

"But continue thou in the things which thou hast learned and hast been assured of, knowing of whom thou hast learned them." Paul was thinking of Timothy's instruction in his home, as well as that which he had received from Paul and others of his companions who had been fellow laborers in the gospel. In those early days there was no such thing as a Bible Institute or a Theological Seminary where young men, who wanted to give themselves wholly to the work of the Lord, could go in order to be trained for Christian service. The custom was for an experienced servant of Christ to take one or more young men with him and instruct them in Scripture and train them in the work of the Lord. This was Timothy's case. He had gone forth with Paul, had heard him preach the truth of the gospel, and had learned from him that which he had gotten direct from God Himself through divine revelation.

Then Timothy had his Bible, and he was responsible to read it. Paul says, "From a child thou hast known the holy scriptures." It is a wonderful thing to know the Holy Scripture from childhood. Many of us can thank God that we first learned to reverence and love the Bible in our own homes. How we should praise Him for godly parents who loved this Book and who implanted in our hearts a reverence for its teachings. Timothy had this privilege. If any of you parents do not give this privilege to your children, you are robbing them of something they will never be able to get anywhere else. Do not depend upon sending your children to others to teach them; do not depend upon the Sunday school or the church service to do this for them. These, of course, are important, but you should supplement this work by instruction in the home.

Timothy was well furnished. He knew the Word of God from a child. It was not, however, the New Testament which the Apostle had in mind. That had not been written when Timothy was a child. Do not neglect the Old Testament. Many Christians do. Many give very little time to the Old Testament, and the result is that they have a very imperfect understanding of the New Testament, for the roots of the New Testament go deep down into the Old Testament. Timothy knew the Hebrew Scriptures. He was familiar with the prophecies concerning the coming of Messiah, so that when the Lord Jesus was presented to him, he was prepared to believe in Him. "From a child thou hast known the holy scriptures, which are able to make thee wise unto salvation through faith which is in Christ Jesus."

Simply knowing Scripture will not produce salvation. One may know the Bible, one may be able to quote many Scripture passages, but that in itself does not save. But the Bible reveals Christ, and when one believes in Him, he is saved. That is what happened in Timothy's case, and thank God, in the experience of millions more.

Note how fully Scripture meets every need for the believer as he goes through this scene. "All scripture is given by inspiration of God." Originally this term *scripture* was applied specifically to the Old Testament. Later the books of the New Testament were likewise so designated. In the last chapter of his Second Epistle the apostle Peter adds Paul's letters to the other Scripture passages.

"All scripture is given by inspiration of God"—that is, it is divinely breathed. The men who wrote the Bible did not write their own thoughts. They wrote as guided by and directed by the Holy Spirit. We read, "No prophecy of the scripture is of any private interpretation. For the prophecy came not in old time by the will of man: but holy men of God spake as they were moved by the Holy Ghost" (2 Peter 1:20–21). Whether it be the historical books of the Bible; or the poetical books, like the Psalms; or the wisdom literature, like Proverbs and Ecclesiastes; or the Gospels and the Epistles of the New Testament, the writers of all these books wrote not simply their own thoughts, but they wrote as they were moved by the Holy Spirit of God. As we turn to any page of this Book we may know that God is speaking to us. "All scripture is given by inspiration of God, and is profitable." One might not think there is much that is profitable or instructive in some parts of the Word, such as the genealogies, for instance, but all are of value, whether we realize it or not.

Scripture is profitable for four things: "for doctrine, for reproof, for correction, for instruction in righteousness." First, it is "profitable for doctrine." The only authoritative book on divine teaching is this blessed volume. Men have written thousands of books to try to explain the Bible, but the Bible itself is the only authority. No matter what teaching may be set forth, if it is not found in the Bible then we are not to accept it. We are to test everything by what is written here.

Second, Scripture is "profitable . . . for reproof." It is profitable to show where we are wrong in our lives and in our thoughts.

Third, it is "profitable . . . for correction." It shows how to get right.

In the fourth place, it is "profitable . . . for instruction in righteousness." After I have taken the right path, it shows me what God's will is for me. Therefore, we shall never reach the place where we can be independent of the Word of God. Sometimes just one verse will change one's whole viewpoint. We need to read and ponder every word in dependence on the Holy Spirit that He may open our understanding to the truth.

As we learn from Scripture, we shall find that it is all-sufficient to so guide and direct "that the man of God may be perfect [or mature], throughly furnished unto all good works."

In the light of this passage we may be sure that nothing is esteemed by God as a good work if it is contrary to the Word of God. When we stand at the judgment seat of Christ, it will not be a question of what we thought about this or that, but what God said. The standard is His Word, not our understanding of it. But we should seek to understand it as the Spirit of God opens it up to us in order that we may walk in obedience to it. If any turn aside from the Word, they will be held responsible for disobedience. The Bible, and the Bible alone, is the basis of instruction and guidance for the Spirit-led believer. God grant that we may be subject to that blessed Word.

CHAPTER 8

Paul's Last Charge to Timothy

2 Timothy 4:1–5

> I charge thee therefore before God, and the Lord Jesus Christ, who shall judge the quick and the dead at his appearing and his kingdom; preach the word; be instant in season, out of season; reprove, rebuke, exhort with all long suffering and doctrine. For the time will come when they will not endure sound doctrine; but after their own lusts shall they heap to themselves teachers, having itching ears; and they shall turn away their ears from the truth, and shall be turned unto fables. But watch thou in all things, endure afflictions, do the work of an evangelist, make full proof of thy ministry. (vv. 1–5)

As we read this letter we need to remind ourselves again and again that it came from one who was about to die for Christ's sake, a man who was under no delusion as to his future. He knew that within a little while he would end his long career at the executioner's block, yet there was no fear on his part, no regrets that he had given himself to that ministry which was to close so tragically, as far as this world is concerned.

He wrote this letter, as we have seen, to one whom he loved, whom he had the privilege of leading to Christ many years before, and who had then gone out with him in the Lord's work and was now ministering in various places where Paul himself had labored for some time. He does not for a moment intimate to the younger preacher that perhaps, after all, it would be better not to give oneself so drastically to the work of the Lord, not to be so self-sacrificing—that perhaps it would be better to compromise to some extent, and thus avoid persecution for Christ's name's sake. No, there is nothing like that in Paul's exhortation to Timothy. He exhorts him to endure his share of suffering and persecution for Christ's sake. It is a poor kind of Christianity that rejoices in the fact that Christ has purchased for us eternal life through His death on the cross, yet refuses to identify oneself with Him in suffering and persecution.

Here we have the Apostle's last charge to the younger preacher. Notice the things he stresses: "I charge thee therefore before God," who in infinite grace had sent His Son to redeem sinners to Himself, "and the Lord Jesus Christ," whose Timothy was and whom he served. Notice how he gives our blessed Savior His full title. He is Lord. He is Jesus. He is the Savior. He is the Anointed of God the Father, "who shall judge the quick and the dead [the living and the dead] at his appearing and his kingdom," or as it might be rendered, "and by his appearing and his kingdom."

Believers are to look forward to the appearing of our Lord Jesus Christ. At that time He is going to give rewards to those who have labored for Him down here, who have been ready to suffer with and for Him, and have held the things of this world with a loose hand while fixing their affection on things above. "When Christ, who is our life, shall appear, then shall ye also appear with him in glory" (Col. 3:4).

In both the Old and New Testaments we have promises of the coming kingdom. That golden age is still in the future to be ushered in when the Lord Jesus returns from heaven in power and glory, to put down iniquity, and to reign over this lower universe for a thousand wonderful years. This is the kingdom for which we pray when we join together in saying, "Thy kingdom come," when, "Thy will shall be done on earth as it is in heaven."

So it is in view of the appearing of our Lord Jesus Christ and the setting up of His kingdom that Paul stresses the importance of faithfulness to Christ while we await the fulfillment of His promise.

He says to Timothy first of all, "Preach the word." He did not tell him to preach philosophy, nor preach politics, nor preach some system of morals, but *preach the Word!* And that takes in the entire Bible, for our commission is not only to preach the gospel that tells us how lost sinners may be saved, but we are to proclaim the whole truth of God which not only gives us the way of salvation but also shows how we ought to live after we are redeemed. The servant of

Christ who preaches the Word will never be at a loss for subjects, for he has the whole Bible from which to choose.

There are many ministers of Christ who have never learned that it is their business to preach the entire Word, and they are always trying to think up topics that may thrill, charm, and entertain the people. But the servant of God is not called to do these things. He is to seek to make people acquainted with the mind of God, to preach the gospel to the unsaved, to show them their lost condition, and then to set before them the remedy that God has provided. He is to open up God's Word to Christian people, showing them how they may be kept from sin and live daily in this life to the glory of God. This is the charge of the Holy Spirit to every minister of the gospel: Preach the Word! He who does this may never be highly esteemed among men as a great orator or declaimer, but he should not mind that. His one object should be to glorify God in setting forth His truth in the way He Himself directs.

Observe the next charge: "Be instant in season, out of season." Paul is really saying, "Be constantly on the lookout for opportunities to glorify God and to make Him known to others." You remember when William Haslam, that English church clergyman, was converted. He preached with such power that he won every member in his own parish to Christ. There was not a person living in the Baldhu section of Cornwall who had not confessed the Lord. Then he became greatly concerned about his neighbors, so he began preaching in adjoining parishes and winning souls there. The other ministers became upset over it, and sent in their objections to the Bishop, saying, "Mr. Haslam is interfering with our work. He is poaching in our parishes, telling our people that they have to be converted and need to be born again."

The Bishop sent for William Haslam and said, "I understand you are preaching all the time. You don't seem to be doing anything else."

William Haslam replied, "My lord bishop, I assure you I preach only in two seasons of the year."

"Oh," said the Bishop, "I am glad to know that. And what seasons are they?"

"In season and out of season," replied William Haslam.

That is the charge that comes to everyone of us if we really know Christ. It is not just for official proclaiming of the Word, not just for pastors and elders, but for all Christians. Let us be instant in season and out of season in winning precious souls to the Lord Jesus Christ.

Then there will be occasions when we will have to "reprove, rebuke, exhort." The last word has really the thought of comfort. So we are to comfort those who need help, assuring those who have sinned of pardon and restoration if they will turn to the blessed Lord and make confession of their failures and wrongdoing. But we must do this with all longsuffering and tenderness. The preacher of grace must not behave in an ungracious manner. I am afraid that when many of us try to reprove we get in a bad spirit ourselves and forget that the servant of the Lord should not strive, but should be characterized by longsuffering, by patience, by tender consideration even of those whom he has to rebuke or reprove.

Note the emphasis put upon teaching sound doctrine. Some people say, "I am not interested in doctrine. I like practical preaching not doctrine." But we need to know the great truths of Scripture in order that we may learn how to behave in accordance with the revelation God has given. Sincerity of purpose is not enough. We are to be sanctified by the truth. David prayed, "Order my steps in thy word" (Ps. 119:133). We must know the Word in order that our lives may be as God would have them. The servant of Christ is therefore responsible to give out sound teaching.

The Apostle knew that the day would come when people would not want this kind of ministry, when they would prefer to hear smooth things. He says, "For the time will come when they will not endure sound doctrine; but after their own lusts shall they heap to themselves teachers, having itching ears." It is not that the *teachers* have itching ears. The teachers in this instance generally have itching palms! They are in the business for filthy lucre. But the *people* have itching ears. They want preachers who will say things to them that will not trouble their consciences but will tickle their fancy.

I never feel worried when people write me letters, saying, "I resent your personal attack on me last Sunday." They always come from people I do not know. If I do know something bad about a person, I am careful never to refer to it in a public address. I would rather see him privately. But every little while I receive a letter, saying, "I don't like your preaching, and I don't think you had any right to expose me in the way you did. I don't know who has been talking to you about me." And they always end up by saying, "It is not true." So whatever made them think I was talking about them, I do not know. I am never concerned about such letters, for when the preacher presents God's Word it is bound to speak to some people. You remember what Sam Jones said, "If you throw a stone into a pack of dogs and one of them yelps, you know who got hit."

We should so walk before God and so live in fellowship with God that the Holy Spirit can speak directly through us. Many will not like this kind of preaching because they have itching ears. They want people to say nice things to them so that they can go away feeling good.

Then we read, "They shall turn away their ears from the truth, and shall be turned unto fables." Some years ago two gentlemen were sitting opposite one another in a railway car. One was reading his Bible. The other looked across and said, "Pardon me. Is that a Bible you are reading?"

The man looked up and said, "Yes, this is the Bible, God's Word."

"Well, well," said the other, "that really astonishes me. You look to me like an intelligent man. I didn't know that intelligent persons ever read the Bible anymore. I used to believe in that when I was a child, but after I became somewhat educated I found there was nothing to it. I believe the day will soon come when civilized people will have no more confidence in the Bible than they have in the old idea of ghosts."

This Christian gentleman looked up quietly and said, "You may be right, but when the day comes that people no longer believe in the Bible they will believe in ghosts again!"

And we see the evidence of that on every hand. People turn away from the truth and take up with—what? With Spiritism, Theosophy, and all kinds of other weird systems and strange cults. They turn away from the truth to satanic doctrines that lead men down to perdition.

Paul says to Timothy, "Watch thou in all things." The Christian life is a warfare. We are in conflict with three enemies: the world, the flesh, and the Devil. We need to be on our guard continually, watching in all things. "Endure affliction," that is, be willing to suffer for faithfulness to the truth.

Must I be carried to the skies
On flowery beds of ease,
While others fought to win the prize
And sailed through bloody seas?

He adds, "Do the work of an evangelist." Now I do not think Timothy was an evangelist. I think, as I read over the passages of Scripture that give information regarding the character of his work, that he was a pastor. He had a shepherd's heart. He cared for the sheep and the lambs of Christ's flock. But Paul says to him, "Do not forget the gospel. Men are dying in their sins. Do not be so occupied with feeding the flock that you overlook the need of those who are out of Christ. Do the work of an evangelist." Some ministers say, "I don't feel I have any evangelistic gift, so I never preach to the unsaved." It is not necessary to have any special gift to preach to the unsaved. Just give them what God says in His Word about the salvation He has provided in the Lord Jesus Christ.

The last exhortation is, "Make full proof of thy ministry." In other words, Paul is saying to Timothy, "Do not be halfhearted, Timothy, and do not be content with halfway measures. Give your whole soul, all your strength, all your ability, all your talents, all your heart, your whole life to the great work to which God has called you."

Although these words were addressed directly to Timothy, they have been preserved by the Spirit of God Himself in order that they may come home to everyone of us, that we may seek to act upon them in our day and generation even as he was responsible to do in his.

CHAPTER 9

PAUL'S VALEDICTORY

2 Timothy 4:6–8

> For I am now ready to be offered, and the time of my departure is at hand. I have fought a good fight, I have finished my course, I have kept the faith: henceforth there is laid up for me a crown of righteousness, which the Lord, the righteous judge, shall give me at that day: and not to me only, but unto all them also that love his appearing. (vv. 6–8)

We may well call this "Paul's Valedictory." Someone has designated it as "Paul's Swan Song." I think I quite understand what he meant. But, personally, I do not feel like speaking of it in that way. You know they say—it is an old fable—that the swan is silent all its life, but opens its bill and begins to sing just as it is dying. I have never been present at the death of any swan, and so I could not witness to the truth of this. But Paul did not wait until death to start singing. From the time he was saved by God's grace, he had a song in his heart which he continued to sing all his life. The night he was in prison in Philippi with his companion, Silas, they both sang praises unto God, even though their feet were fast in the stocks and their backs terribly lacerated by the cruel flogging they had received. Paul said, "I will sing with the spirit, and I will sing with the understanding also" (1 Cor. 14:15). He did not begin to sing just as he was about to die.

This letter has peculiar interest. It is Paul's final message, not only to his young friend Timothy, but also to the church as a whole. We should remember some of the circumstances under which these words were written. The Apostle was now an old man. He had been preaching the gospel for over thirty years, perhaps about thirty-five years. He had been confined for some months in the Mamertine Prison in Rome. There is no window in that prison where he could get a whiff of fresh air, just a hole in the roof through which they dropped whatsoever food they cared to give him, and through which water was lowered down to him. As I stood there I noticed a cleft in the floor, and you could look down and see the dark water of the river rolling beneath the cell. From that foul and dismal dungeon Paul sent forth this glad, triumphant message.

He was a lonely man. He tells us farther on in the chapter of one after another who had left him, going out to minister the gospel in various places. "Demas," he says, "hath forsaken me, having loved this present world. . . . Only Luke"—faithful Dr. Luke, whom Paul called elsewhere, "The beloved physician" (Col. 4:14)—"only Luke is with me." Luke remained with him to the last no doubt, ministering in every way that circumstances permitted.

Under such circumstances you might forgive a man if he were discouraged and disheartened, and if, looking back upon his long years of service, he felt that God had not fully appreciated what he had done. But Paul had no such thoughts as these. He says, "I am now ready to be offered," literally, *poured out.* In writing to the Philippians, he says, "Yea, and if I be offered [or, poured out] upon the sacrifice and service of your faith, I joy, and rejoice with you all" (2:17). The reference is to the drink offering. If the burnt offering was a sheep or a lamb, the parts were placed upon the fire on the altar, and the priest took a flagon of wine and poured it out upon that which was to be burnt. This was called the drink offering. It symbolized our blessed Lord Jesus pouring out His soul unto death for our redemption on Calvary.

Paul was to drink of the same cup. So he says, "For I am now ready to be offered." He was ready to yield up his life, for it belonged to Christ; He had saved him and now Paul was glad to die for Him. That is really what he meant. He adds, "The time of *my* departure is at hand"; literally, "The time of my dissolution is at hand." The hour was near when his spirit was to be separated from his body, to depart and be with Christ. He did not mean merely that the time of going out of the world was nigh, but rather the time of the separation of spirit and body. In 2 Corinthians 5:1 he says, "For we know that if our earthly house of this tabernacle were dissolved, we have a building of God, an house not made with hands, eternal in the heavens." He speaks of dwelling in this body while living, and going out of the body in the hour of death. At death the Christian goes out of the body and goes home to be forever with the Lord. So Paul says, "The hour of my dissolution [the end of present conditions] is at hand."

Then as he looked back over scores of conflicts with unseen powers in heavenly places, the world-rulers of this darkness, of which he speaks in the epistle to the Ephesians, he was able to say, "I have fought the good fight." It is not exactly as we have it in our King James Version, "I have fought *a* good fight." To say that would be to pass on his own ability as a fighter, as though to say: "I have done very well; I have fought a good fight." What he really said is this, "I have fought the good contest." He was on the right side in the conflict. Some of us may feel that we have not done very well as Christian soldiers, but at any rate, we will be able to thank God in that day that we were on the right side. We were on Christ's side in the war against iniquity and unrighteousness. That is what Paul means, "I have fought the good fight."

"I have finished my course." In the twentieth chapter of the book of Acts, where Paul addressed the Ephesian elders, perhaps some six years before he wrote this letter, he told the elders that his one great concern was to finish his course with joy (v. 24). He had run well by the grace of God for nearly thirty years since that day he met the Lord on the Damascus turnpike. His earnest desire was to finish well. He did not want to break near the end. Oh, how many have fought a good fight for years and then in some way, even in old age when we think one should be free from temptations, they have been broken down, perhaps because of self-confidence! They have gotten their eyes off the Lord. Some who made a good record for many years have had a dishonorable old age.

I will never forget, as a boy, how I used to be amazed as I heard an old preacher say in public prayer, "O Lord, keep my eyes on the Lord Jesus. Don't let me become a wicked old man." I used to wonder why he prayed like that, but I have since seen many who had a testimony for Christ in their early days break down and become wicked old men because they got their eyes off Christ.

I am not talking about losing one's soul. I am talking about our lives counting for Christ here in this world, and the danger of losing one's testimony for Him.

"I have kept the faith." God grant that everyone of us who confess the name of Jesus may be able to say that when we come to the end—"I have kept the faith!"

Some years ago a fearful railroad wreck took dreadful toll of life and limb in an eastern state. A train, loaded with young people returning from school, was stalled on a suburban track because of what is known as a "hot box." The Limited was soon due, but a flagman was sent back to warn the engineer in order to avert a rear-end collision. Thinking all was well, the crowd laughed and chatted while the train hands worked on in fancied security. Suddenly the whistle of the Limited was heard, and on came the heavy train and crashed into the local, with horrible effect.

The engineer of the Limited saved his own life by jumping, and some days afterward was hailed into court to account for his part in the calamity. And now a curious discrepancy in testimony occurred. He was asked, "Did you not see the flagman warning you to stop?"

He replied, "I saw him, but he waved a yellow flag, and I took it for granted all was well, and so went on, though slowing down."

The flagman was called. "What flag did you wave?"

"A red flag, but he went by me like a shot."

"Are you sure it was red?"

"Absolutely."

Both insisted on the correctness of their testimony, and it was demonstrated that neither was color-blind. Finally the man was asked to produce the flag itself as evidence. After some delay he was able to do so, and then the mystery was explained. *It had been red,* but it had been exposed to the weather so long that all the red was bleached out, and it was but *a dirty yellow!* Oh, the lives eternally wrecked by the yellow gospels of the day—the bloodless theories of unregenerate men who send their hearers to their doom instead of stopping them on their downward road!

No wonder the faithful Apostle cries, "Though we, or an angel from heaven, preach any other gospel unto you than that which we have preached unto you, let him be accursed" (Gal. 1:8). And lest any should think he spoke in haste, not weighing his words, he adds, "As we said before, so say I now again, if any man preach any other gospel unto you than that ye have received, let him be accursed" (Gal. 1:9). To trifle with souls is an awful sin.

How many there are who once bore a faithful testimony and proclaimed salvation through the precious blood of our Lord Jesus Christ, but who, after some years have gone on, have failed to carry out the commission given to them, and their message is no longer that of the blood of Christ. It is a dirty yellow flag of man's personal acceptability to God on the ground of his own character and good works, and the result is that many are being lured on to their eternal doom.

There is no other real message than that of the cross. "Without [the] shedding of blood [there] is no remission." "The blood of Jesus Christ [God's] Son cleanseth us from all sin." When we get home, the blood will be the theme of our song for eternity. "They sung a new song," says John, "saying, Thou art worthy . . . for thou wast slain, and hast redeemed us to God by thy blood out of every kindred, and tongue, and people, and nation" (Rev. 5:9).

Paul had kept the faith, and now he says, "Henceforth there is laid up for me a crown of righteousness, which the Lord, the righteous judge, shall give me at that day: and not to me only, but unto all them also that love his appearing." In 1 Corinthians he speaks of crowns and rewards. The crown is to be distinguished from salvation. The crown speaks of approval; salvation is by grace through faith, but rewards are for service. Our blessed Lord, the righteous Judge, will give rewards for the work done in the body. So Paul, in 1 Corinthians 9:27, says, "I keep under my body, and bring it into subjection: lest that by any means, when I have preached to others, I myself should be a castaway." Or, literally, should be set to one side; should fail of the reward. He draws an illustration from the arena. How carefully young men train that they might receive the prize. He says, "They do it to obtain a corruptible crown; but we an incorruptible" (1 Cor. 9:25). And so through the years he had kept a prayerful watch that he might not allow himself to give way to the desires of the flesh. He did not allow the body to dominate, but, he says, "I keep under my body, and bring it into subjection." Instead of permitting his body to master him, he mastered it. At the end of the race he could say, "Henceforth there is laid up for me a crown of righteousness, which the Lord, the righteous judge, shall give me at that day."

There is a difference between the gift of righteousness and the crown of righteousness. Every believer in the Lord Jesus Christ receives the gift of righteousness. All of us are made the righteousness of God in Christ. We have no righteousness of our own. That which we fancy to be our righteousness is but as filthy rags in God's sight. When we believe in the Lord Jesus, our faith is imputed to us for righteousness, and we stand before God cleared of every charge. That is our justification. That is perfect. That is complete. But the crown of righteousness is something quite different. It is the reward that is given to those who have lived righteous lives as they have waited expectantly for the coming of the Lord Jesus Christ. So Paul says, "Henceforth there is laid up for me a crown of righteousness, which the Lord, the righteous judge, shall give me at that day." The Lord, the righteous Judge, will sit on the judgment seat where the works of believers will be examined.

This is different from the Great White Throne where the unsaved are to be judged. We find the expression "the day of Christ," and sometimes, "the day of Jesus Christ," and in one place, "the day of our Lord Jesus Christ." These terms always refer to the time when "the Lord himself shall descend from heaven with a shout, with the voice of the archangel, and with the trump of God: and the dead in Christ shall rise first: then we which are alive and remain shall be caught up together with them in the clouds, to meet the Lord in the air" (1 Thess. 4:16–17). Then we shall stand before His judgment seat. That will be the day when we will give account of the deeds done in the body.

Observe that expression, "deeds done in the body." I do not know of any Scripture that promises reward for post-mortem gifts for the work of the Lord. There are some who accumulate vast fortunes, forgetting the Lord's warning about laying up treasure on earth. Then when they are about to die they bequeath their wealth to Christian enterprises. It is far better to give what you can while in the body, for if given as unto the Lord this assures reward in that day.

If you have money you are not going to need, put it to work while you are in the body. To do it for Jesus' sake is to assure a reward in that day.

Paul adds, "And not to me only, but unto all them also that love his appearing." He is not thinking of himself only. He was not the only one who will have a crown of righteousness. It is for all them also that love Christ's appearing. Do you love His appearing? Are you waiting for the coming of the Lord Jesus Christ? Is that the lodestar of your soul? We read, "Every man that hath this hope in him purifieth himself, even as he is pure" (1 John 3:3). The hope of the coming of the Lord is the most sanctifying thing I know. If you are living day by day as one expecting the early return of your Lord, you are not going to be carried away by the trend of the times. You are not going to yield to the solicitations of the world, the flesh, and the Devil.

May God grant that in that day not one of us will come up empty-handed; that not one of us will have to look back with regret upon years that might have been lived to the glory of God but were not, or upon hoarded wealth that might have been put to use for Christ!

CHAPTER 10

LUKE AND DEMAS

2 Timothy 4:9–22

Do thy diligence to come shortly unto me: for Demas hath forsaken me, having loved this present world, and is departed unto Thessalonica; Crescens to Galatia, Titus unto Dalmatia. Only Luke is with me. Take Mark, and bring him with thee: for he is profitable to me for the ministry. And Tychicus have I sent to Ephesus. The cloke that I left at Troas with Carpus, when thou comest, bring with thee, and the books, but especially the parchments. Alexander the coppersmith did me much evil: the Lord reward him according to his works: of whom be thou ware also; for he hath greatly withstood our words. At my first answer no man stood with me, but all men forsook me: I pray God that it may not be laid to their charge. Notwithstanding the Lord stood with me, and strengthened me; that by me the preaching might be fully known, and that all the Gentiles might hear: and I was delivered out of the mouth of the lion. And the Lord shall deliver me from every evil work, and will preserve me unto his heavenly kingdom: to whom be glory for ever and ever. Amen. Salute Prisca and Aquila, and the household of Onesiphorus. Erastus abode at Corinth: but Trophimus have I left at Miletum sick. Do thy diligence to come before winter. Eubulus greeteth

> thee, and Pudens, and Linus, and Claudia, and all the brethren. The Lord Jesus Christ be with thy spirit. Grace be with you. Amen. (vv. 9–22)

A section such as this might not seem to have very much in it that is for real spiritual edification, and one might ask whether divine inspiration was needed to give us these greetings and salutations. But God had a special reason for causing the Apostle to put these things into his letters. In the first place, in order that they might be preserved for our instruction and help in a future day, and then to enable us to understand the circumstances in which Paul found himself at this time much better than we otherwise could.

We have noticed that Paul wrote this particular letter during his second imprisonment, while awaiting execution as a martyr for Christ's sake. He was anxious to see his friend, Timothy, to whom this letter is written, once more before his impending death. So he urged him, in verse 9, to do his "diligence to come shortly unto" him. A little farther down, in verse 21, Paul says, "Do thy diligence to come before winter." This might have a double suggestion. Possibly he already knew that he was to be martyred that winter, or because the cold weather was near at hand he wanted Timothy to bring him the needed supplies that would help to make the winter in an underground dungeon more comfortable.

Then he spoke sorrowfully of one of his former companions: "For Demas hath forsaken me, having loved this present world, and is departed unto Thessalonica." He also mentioned two other associates who had gone away on evangelistic tours: "Crescens to Galatia, Titus unto Dalmatia." Luke, the beloved physician, remained with him, as we are told in verse 11, "Only Luke is with me."

Then there is a very interesting request: "Take Mark, and bring him with thee: for he is profitable to me for the ministry." This is the John Mark who went out with Paul and Barnabas on their first missionary journey, but who left them at Perga in Pamphylia and returned to his home in Jerusalem. Paul felt that Mark had manifested a rather poor spirit at that time, and later on when Barnabas wanted to take him on another journey, Paul refused to agree to this, as he considered Mark had proven untrustworthy before. You see, with Paul, a missionary journey was no pleasurable excursion, and he wanted a man who would stay with him, endure the hardship, and not go back home if things became difficult. So he said, "No, we will not take Mark with us." Paul and Barnabas were both very godly men, but this was something on which they could not agree. Barnabas, who was closely related to John Mark, pleaded with Paul to give the boy another chance, but the latter was adamant. So we are told that the contention became so sharp between them that they separated. Barnabas took Mark and returned to Cyprus, while Paul went another way and chose Silas to go with him. God blessed and used both Paul and Barnabas in spite of their difference of opinion, and they were warm friends later on, as we know (1 Cor. 9:6).

As the years went on, we find this difference had passed away. Paul speaks very tenderly and lovingly of Mark, and expressed his desire to see him again.

I am glad that Barnabas gave Mark another chance, for he made good the second time. He went on in the Lord's work, and Paul recognized that God had made Mark a profitable servant. It was he who wrote the second gospel.

Next Paul mentioned Tychicus, who had traveled with him, "Tychicus have I sent to Ephesus."

In verse 13 he says something that is rather interesting: "The cloke that I left at Troas with Carpus, when thou comest, bring with thee, and the books, but especially the parchments." Evidently he had been entertained in the home of a man named Carpus. Just where, we are not told, but he had left his heavy coat there until he should send for it. Now he felt the need of it. He requests also that Timothy bring his books and, especially, some parchments. These parchments may have been simply plain material on which he could write letters, but if they contained parts of Scripture we can well understand why he would be anxious to receive them.

"And the books"—that he might pass the time profitably in prison. Here I am reminded of what Francis Newman said of that devoted servant of God, J. N. Darby: "Never before had I seen a man so resolved that no word of the New Testament should be a dead letter to him. I once said, 'But do you really think that no part of the New Testament may have been temporary in its object? For instance, what should we have lost if St. Paul had never written, "The cloke that I left at Troas . . . bring with thee, and the books, but especially the parchments"?' He answered with the greatest promptitude, 'I should have lost something, for it was exactly that verse which alone saved me from selling my little library. No! Every word, depend upon it, is from the Spirit, and is for eternal service.'"

"Alexander the coppersmith did me much evil: the Lord reward him according to his works: of whom be thou ware also; for he hath greatly withstood our words." This may have been the same Alexander referred to elsewhere, whom Paul had delivered unto Satan, because he was leading the believers into false teachings (1 Tim. 1:20). As Paul looked back over his first appearance before Nero, he said, "At my first answer no man stood with me, but all men forsook me: I pray God that it may not be laid to their charge." Think of that: the aged apostle charged with sedition against the Roman Empire, standing there alone before Caesar. No one to take his part. No one to say, "I know this man. I know him to be a man of uprightness and integrity, and I heartily endorse his message." But there he stood, alone, faithfully witnessing to the truth of God. Did I say alone? No, he was not alone. He himself said, "Notwithstanding the Lord stood with me, and strengthened me; that by me the preaching might be fully known, and that all the Gentiles might hear: and I was delivered out of the mouth of the lion." In a little while he was to die for Christ's sake, but he could say with confidence, "And the Lord shall deliver me from every evil work, and will preserve me unto his heavenly kingdom: to whom be glory for ever and ever. Amen."

Then the letter concludes with several salutations. "Salute Prisca and Aquila, and the household of Onesiphorus." Priscilla and Aquila were friends of Paul's with whom he had lived in Corinth and Ephesus. They had given him a home when he had none of his own. "And the household of Onesiphorus." He had spoken of how this man had sought him out (1:16–18). His household is mentioned here. One of his companions, Erastus, remained at Corinth. "But Trophimus have I left at Miletum sick." Paul was forced to leave this brother behind because of illness. Some people think that Christians should never be sick, and if they are, it is because of their unfaithfulness to the Lord. But Paul had to leave his sick companion at Miletum, and there is no indication of unfaithfulness here. Neither did Paul heal him. Healing from sickness is not always God's will for the Christian.

Then we have that word, "Do thy diligence to come before winter." He next mentioned several who sent greetings: Eubulus, Pudens, Linus, and Claudia. Linus is listed in Roman Catholic chronology as the second bishop of Rome. Peter was supposed to be the first. But neither Linus nor Peter knew anything about it, you may be sure of that! Paul then closes the letter with the words, "The Lord Jesus Christ be with thy spirit. Grace be with you. Amen."

Now, having glanced briefly at this portion, I am going back to note what is said about Demas and Luke. "For Demas hath forsaken me, having loved this present world. . . . Only Luke is with me."

These two names had been linked together in other Epistles. In Colossians 4:14 we read, "Luke, the beloved physician, and Demas, greet you." Then in the little epistle to Philemon, in verse 24, these two names are mentioned with others, "Marcus, Aristarchus, Demas, Lucas, my fellowlabourers." It is very evident that both Luke and Demas were very good friends of the apostle Paul. He counted on them. They worked with him, traveled with him, no doubt relieving him of a great many responsibilities.

Here we read, "Only Luke is with me." Luke remained faithful to the end. He was found by Paul in Troas, as we gather from the book of Acts. Luke may have been a Greek-speaking Jew; on the other hand, he might have been a Gentile. There is no evidence either way. If a Gentile, then he is the only New Testament Gentile writer, for all the rest were Jews, Hebrew Christians. The word *Luke* means "light." He was a scientific man, a physician, a man of culture and refinement. He had investigated Christianity very carefully before accepting it. The introduction to his gospel tells us that he had looked into these things that had been reported concerning Jesus. He gives considerable detailed information regarding the virgin birth of our Lord. Matthew simply mentions that His mother was a virgin in accordance with the prophecy in Isaiah, but Luke gives many particulars that evidence the physician's personal conversation with Mary.

From the time when he met Paul at Troas until Paul's death, Luke was always closely linked with him. At different times in the book of Acts we see that he remained behind when Paul went on, doubtless to help build up young converts. Then he would join Paul later.

Not once does Luke mention his own name either in his gospel or in the book of Acts, and he wrote both of these. But in the Acts we are able to know when Luke is on the scene and when he is not. If he is with Paul, he uses the pronouns "we" and "us." If he is not with Paul's party, he uses "they" and "them." Then when he rejoins them, it is "we" and "us" again. In this way we can trace his journeys with Paul in the latter chapters of the book. He was faithful to the end, and what a crown there will be for him in that coming day!

About this other man, Demas, we know very little. He and Luke must have been very intimate. We get this from the way their names are found together in these two Scripture passages. Now Paul is in prison, and Demas must have said, "This business of preaching the gospel isn't going to pan out very well." So he did not know whether he could go on or not, and by-and-by, after careful consideration, he determined to leave Paul and return to the world.

Paul says, "Demas hath forsaken me." He does not say that Demas has forsaken God or given up his faith in the Lord Jesus Christ, but that "Demas hath forsaken me." There is nothing to indicate that he gave up faith in the gospel that he professed and became an apostate. There is no intimation that he plunged into a life of sin. But he turned away from Paul, having loved this present world. He was more concerned about temporal things than he was about getting a reward at the judgment seat of Christ, and therefore his name goes down on the page of Holy Scripture as a warning to every servant of Christ.

We remember the words of our Lord Jesus, "No man, having put his hand to the plough, and looking back, is fit for the kingdom of God" (Luke 9:62). Demas lost his great opportunity. He might have been honored of God as a wonderful soul winner, but he loved this present world.

May that speak to everyone of our hearts. It is only as we are occupied with Christ Himself that we are set free from the love of the world. The Spirit of God says to every Christian, "Love not the world, neither the things that are in the world. If any man love the world, the love of the Father is not in him. For all that is in the world, the lust of the flesh, and the lust of the eyes, and the pride of life, is not of the Father, but is of the world. And the world passeth away, and the lust thereof: but he that doeth the will of God abideth for ever" (1 John 2:15–17).

May we be encouraged by Luke and warned by Demas to go on faithfully in the path of service to which our God has called us. God grant that it will never be said of any us that we "loved this present world." And if I am speaking to any who have never come to Christ, oh, I plead with you, make the choice that Luke made. If you are troubled by doubt and perplexity, then study Scripture for yourself. Look for the evidences of the truth in the Word of God itself, and look for corroborative evidence in the lives of those who have received Christ. See what wonderful things God has done for them. Put your faith in Jesus, and so go on with us to yonder glory-land.

PART 3

Titus

CHAPTER 1

INTRODUCTION

There are four letters addressed to individuals which the Holy Spirit indicted through the apostle Paul. Three are called pastoral, because directed to young preachers, exhorting them to diligence in their calling. The fourth, to Philemon, is decidedly personal.

While the two letters to Timothy and that to Titus are in some respects alike, there is this marked difference: to Timothy the apostle stresses the importance of sound doctrine, whereas to Titus he dwells on sound behavior. In other words, the subject of this epistle is, "The truth which is according to godliness."

Never was there a time when the necessity of practical piety was so marked as in the days in which our lot is cast. Loose doctrine makes for loose living. On the other hand, it is quite possible to contend earnestly for fundamental principles when the life is anything but consistent with the profession.

Titus was a Greek, as Paul tells us, who accompanied him to Jerusalem to discuss the Gentiles' relation to the law of Moses. A trustworthy man apparently, for to him was committed the responsibility of a collection among the Gentile assemblies for the relief of the famine-stricken Jewish brethren in Palestine. Paul speaks approvingly of Titus' general behavior, and yet significantly adds, "With Titus I sent a brother." He would allow nothing to cast disparagement upon a servant of God in money matters. In this we see an important lesson for ourselves.

When Paul wrote this epistle Titus was in the island of Crete and was what we might call an apostolic legate to whom was committed the work of organizing the churches of Crete. The letter was evidently written between Paul's two imprisonments, for we have no record of his having been in Crete prior to the first imprisonment, nor of his later wintering at Nicopolis. But evidently after he was freed from the charges brought against him by the Jerusalem Jews, he went about, as tradition declares, continuing his ministry until arrested a second time. It was during this interval that he went with Titus to Crete, later leaving the younger man to complete the work while he moved on to other parts.

The three chapters of the epistle are its natural divisions. Chapter 1 dwells upon the need of godliness in the church; chapter 2, godliness in the home; and chapter 3, godliness in the world.

CHAPTER 2

Godliness in the Church

Titus 1:1–16

> Paul, a servant of God, and an apostle of Jesus Christ, according to the faith of God's elect, and the acknowledging of the truth which is after godliness; in hope of eternal life, which God, that cannot lie, promised before the world began; but hath in due times manifested his word through preaching, which is committed unto me according to the commandment of God our Saviour; to Titus, mine own son after the common faith: Grace, mercy, and peace, from God the Father and the Lord Jesus Christ our Saviour. For this cause left I thee in Crete, that thou shouldest set in order the things that are wanting, and ordain elders in every city, as I had appointed thee: if any be blameless, the husband of one wife, having faithful children not accused of riot or unruly. For a bishop must be blameless, as the steward of God; not self-willed, not soon angry, not given to wine, no striker, not given to filthy lucre; but a lover of hospitality, a lover of good men, sober, just, holy, temperate; holding fast the faithful word as he hath been taught, that he may be able by sound doctrine both to exhort and to convince the gainsayers. For there are many unruly and vain talkers and deceivers, specially they of the circumcision: whose mouths must be stopped, who

> subvert whole houses, teaching things which they ought not, for filthy lucre's sake. One of themselves, even a prophet of their own, said, the Cretians are alway liars, evil beasts, slow bellies. This witness is true. Wherefore rebuke them sharply, that they may be sound in the faith; not giving heed to Jewish fables, and commandments of men, that turn from the truth. Unto the pure all things are pure: but unto them that are defiled and unbelieving is nothing pure; but even their mind and conscience is defiled. They profess that they know God; but in works they deny him, being abominable, and disobedient, and unto every good work reprobate. (vv. 1–16)

Let us look particularly at the first chapter. Verses 1–4 give the salutation. Paul speaks of himself as a bondman of God, and a sent-one of Jesus Christ in accordance with the faith of God's elect. *Faith* here refers not to trust nor confidence in God on the part of the elect but to that body of doctrine which the elect are called to defend. He adds, "And the acknowledging of the truth which is after godliness." *Godliness* is literally "godlikeness," or "piety." The truth apprehended in the soul produces piety in the life. This is insisted on in this letter.

The statement of verse 2 deserves special consideration: "In hope of eternal life, which God, that cannot lie, promised before the world began." It should read, "the age-times," or "the times of the ages," in place of "world." There are two Greek words, not merely one, that are here together translated "world."

The "times of the ages" are the dispensations, the redemptive ages which began after the fall of man. The promise of life here referred to, as also in 2 Timothy 1:1, was the declaration Jehovah made when He cursed the serpent: "And I will put enmity between thee and the woman, and between thy seed and her seed; it shall bruise thy head, and thou shalt bruise his heel" (Gen. 3:15). This is the promise of life. It was not a promise given before the creation of the material universe, but before the ages of time had started to run their course. Sin had come in, but man was not to be left under the sentence of death. A divine Deliverer was to come from God, the Virgin's Son, who would bring in life. In due time God fulfilled this promise, and it is now proclaimed by His Word throughout the world.

From verses 5–9 we have instruction given to Titus in regard to the ordination of elders. He was to set in order the things that were wanting, organizing the churches in a godly way and ordaining elders in every city by apostolic direction. These elders must be blameless, husbands of but one wife, having their households in godly subjection. That *elder* and *bishop* refer to the same person seems evident: "For," he continues, as though speaking of exactly the same class, "a bishop must be blameless, as the steward of God," a man who holds himself in control, not willful, nor of bad temper, self-indulgent, quarrelsome, nor yet covetous, but hospitable, warm of heart toward his brethren, delighting in those who are good, sober, just, holy. He must not play fast and loose with Holy Scripture, but hold fast the Word as he hath been taught, that he may be able by sound doctrine to exhort and convince the gainsayers. Thus in five short verses the apostle portrays for us the ideal elder or bishop. *Elder* suggests a man of maturity, while *bishop* emphasizes his office, the word meaning an "overseer."

The need of godly order in the church was evident. In Crete, as elsewhere, there were many unruly, vain talkers and deceivers, particularly those who had come out of Judaism. Never having been fully delivered from the law, they prated of their greater privileges, and sought to bring the Gentile believers into bondage. "Whose mouths must be stopped, [for they] subvert whole houses, teaching things which they ought not, for filthy lucre's sake." That is, they were seeking to form a party around themselves, having in view their own aggrandizement and enrichment.

These Cretan Jews were like their Gentile fellow countrymen of whom Epimenides had written, "The Cretans are always liars, evil beasts, slow bellies." The last expression might read, "greedy gluttons." What people are by nature comes out even after Christ has wrought in their souls, and therefore calls for greater watchfulness. The old nature is not changed by conversion, though a new nature is given. But the motions of the flesh must be put to death if there would be a life of victory and piety. So Paul commands Titus to rebuke them sharply in order that they may be sound in the faith. They must be warned against Jewish fables and commandments of men (taking the place of revealed truth), which would only lead to apostasy.

The fifteenth verse has frequently been utterly misused: "Unto the pure all things are pure: but unto them that are defiled and unbelieving is nothing pure; but even their mind and conscience is defiled." This does not mean that things which to others are unholy become in themselves pure when done by those of superior mind. It means that the pure delight in purity, even as the unholy delight in that which is impure. With mind and conscience defiled such may make a great religious profession declaring that they know God, but their evil works prove that they are utter strangers to Him. It is against the behavior of such that Titus is called upon to warn the people of God.

CHAPTER 3

Godliness in the Home

Titus 2:1–15

But speak thou the things which become sound doctrine: that the aged men be sober, grave, temperate, sound in faith, in charity, in patience. The aged women likewise, that they be in behaviour as becometh holiness, not false accusers, not given to much wine, teachers of good things; that they may teach the young women to be sober, to love their husbands, to love their children, to be discreet, chaste, keepers at home, good, obedient to their own husbands, that the word of God be not blasphemed. Young men likewise exhort to be sober minded. In all things showing thyself a pattern of good works: in doctrine showing uncorruptness, gravity, sincerity, sound speech, that cannot be condemned; that he that is of the contrary part may be ashamed, having no evil thing to say of you. Exhort servants to be obedient unto their own masters, and to please them well in all things; not answering again; not purloining, but showing all good fidelity; that they may adorn the doctrine of God our Saviour in all things. For the grace of God that bringeth salvation hath appeared to all men, teaching us that, denying ungodliness and worldly lusts, we should live soberly, righteously, and godly, in this present world; looking for that blessed hope, and the glorious appearing of the great God and our Saviour

> Jesus Christ; who gave himself for us, that he might redeem us from all iniquity, and purify unto himself a peculiar people, zealous of good works. These things speak, and exhort, and rebuke with all authority. Let no man despise thee. (vv. 1–15)

Passing from the question of the church, the epistle takes up godliness in the home. Titus is exhorted to speak the things that are in accord with the sound doctrine, or really "the healthful teaching," and in so doing he should counsel the various members of the Christian society. There is a message for aged men and women, young men and women, and also servants.

It is not, however, as in Ephesians and Colossians, a direct exhortation addressed to each of these classes. On the contrary, Titus is instructed as to his own line of procedure to help these various persons to walk consistently with their profession.

The aged men were to be so taught that they would be characterized by sobriety, gravity, self-control, soundness in the faith, love, and patience. The aged women were to walk in accordance with their holy profession, being especially warned against a wrong use of the tongue—"not false accusers." The word is the same as employed for the Devil himself. He is preeminently the slanderer. What a sad thing when Christians so forget their high and holy calling as to be slanderers one of another, thus giving place to the Devil! The aged women are not to become self-indulgent, but to teach, by example as well as precept, those who are younger.

Observe that Titus is not told to instruct the young women personally in regard to their behavior. That might not always be discreet and might compromise him as a servant of Christ. He is to address himself to the aged women and they are to "train" the younger. The word translated *teach* in verse 4 is really "train." The young women are to be trained in sobriety. They are to be taught to love their husbands and their children, and be discreet, chaste, keepers at home. It is really "workers at home"; idleness is not conducive to holiness. They are to be good, or kind, subject to their own husbands, that the Word of God be not blasphemed.

To the young men Titus may address himself directly. He is to exhort them to be sober-minded, but at the same time careful to set an example in all things.

Men will forgive a preacher if he is not eloquent or highly cultured. They will forgive him if he lacks in personal attractiveness or even in wisdom, but they will never forgive him if he is insincere. He who handles holy things must himself live in the power of them. His speech, too, is to be as sound as his life and teaching, in order that those opposed to him may be put to shame when, like the enemies of Daniel, they can find no evil thing to say against him.

In the Revised Version we have "us" instead of "you" at the close of the eighth verse, which might imply that the behavior of Christians would close the mouths of those who desire to find fault with the servants of Christ, through whom they had been led to make a Christian profession.

In verses 9–10 we have the behavior of Christian servants. They are to be obedient to their own masters, to seek to please them well, not answering again, not purloining nor pilfering what is not rightfully their own, but on the other hand showing all good fidelity that thus they may reflect credit on the truth they profess. Integrity and trustworthiness in the little details of their service will glorify the One whose bondmen they really are.

It is to this that we have all been called, as is shown in verses 11–15, "The grace of God, [salvation bringing for all men], hath appeared." A divine message sent from heaven to earth, showing not only that Christ saves us, but teaching us that denying, or refusing, ungodliness and worldly lusts, we should live soberly, righteously and piously in this present world, "looking for that blessed hope, and the appearing of the glory of our great God and Saviour Jesus Christ." This last expression should be translated in this way, according to the judgment of many sober authorities. He is our great God, and it is He who became in grace our Savior.

It is the return of the Lord that is thus put before us to influence our daily lives. It is one thing to hold the doctrine of the Lord's return, but quite another to be held by that blessed hope.

These things Titus is to speak, exhort, and rebuke with all authority.

CHAPTER 4

Godliness in the World

Titus 3:1–15

Put them in mind to be subject to principalities and powers, to obey magistrates, to be ready to every good work, to speak evil of no man, to be no brawlers, but gentle, showing all meekness unto all men. For we ourselves also were sometimes foolish, disobedient, deceived, serving divers lusts and pleasures, living in malice and envy, hateful, and hating one another. But after that the kindness and love of God our Saviour toward man appeared, not by works of righteousness which we have done, but according to his mercy he saved us, by the washing of regeneration, and renewing of the Holy Ghost; which he shed on us abundantly through Jesus Christ our Saviour; that being justified by his grace, we should be made heirs according to the hope of eternal life. This is a faithful saying, and these things I will that thou affirm constantly, that they which have believed in God might be careful to maintain good works. These things are good and profitable unto men. But avoid foolish questions, and genealogies, and contentions, and strivings about the law; for they are unprofitable and vain. A man that is an heretick after the first and second admonition reject; knowing that he that is such is subverted, and sinneth, being condemned of himself. When I shall send Artemas unto thee, or Tychicus, be diligent

> to come unto me to Nicopolis: for I have determined there to winter. Bring Zenas the lawyer and Apollos on their journey diligently, that nothing be wanting unto them. And let ours also learn to maintain good works for necessary uses, that they be not unfruitful. All that are with me salute thee. Greet them that love us in the faith. Grace be with you all. Amen. (vv. 1–15)

In the third chapter we have the Christian's relationship to the world outside. He must not plead heavenly citizenship in order to free himself from his responsibilities as an earthly citizen. The same apostle who wrote to the Philippians, "Our citizenship is in heaven," declared himself a Roman citizen on more than one occasion, and claimed rights thereby.

And so Titus was to teach these restless Cretans to be subject to proper authority, always ready to participate in anything for the good of the community; speaking evil of none, but manifesting the meekness and gentleness of Christ unto all.

This of course does not mean that the Christian is to immerse himself in politics. He will only be defiled if he attempts it, and he will fail in the very thing he is trying to do. Lot could not purify conditions in Sodom by running for office, and many a Christian has found that it was in vain for him to attempt to stem the tide of iniquity by becoming a politician. But the Christian is to set an example of piety in his civic responsibilities. He is to be obedient to law and to pay honestly his taxes, or tribute as the case may be, and to pray for all who are in positions of authority. Then, too, he is to remember the admonition, "[As much as in you is], do good unto all men." Therefore he should be interested in anything which is for the blessing of mankind. This, however, does not leave him at liberty to take part in plans and schemes that are manifestly contrary to the Word of God, even though they may be loudly vaunted as for the upbuilding of humanity. But by generosity, by uprightness of life, and by compassionate interest in his fellows, he is to commend the doctrine of Christ.

It is by such behavior that Christians prove to the world that they are indeed a new creation in Christ Jesus. There was a time when we were like others, "foolish, disobedient, deceived, serving [various unholy desires] and pleasures, living in malice and envy, hateful and hating one another." We were not all guilty to the same extent, but we were all in non-subjection to God, self-willed, and living in disobedience to His Word.

But He in grace undertook our salvation. Not that we became at last so distressed about our sinfulness that we longed after Him, but He in infinite kindness reached down to where we were. "The love of God our Saviour toward man," is literally, "the philanthropy of God."

God is a lover of men, and because He so loved He sent His Son to be the propitiation for our sins. And so we have been saved not through merit of our own—"not by works of righteousness which we have done, but according to his mercy he saved us, by the washing of regeneration, and renewing of the Holy Ghost."

The washing is the application of the Word of God to heart and conscience, thus producing through the Spirit's power, the new nature. Having been thus washed from our old behavior, we are daily being renewed by the Holy Spirit, which God shed on us abundantly through Jesus Christ our Savior.

And God's purpose in thus working on our behalf and in us was that we, being justified by His grace, should be made heirs according to the hope of eternal life.

Every believer has eternal life now as a present possession. Nevertheless, we are exhorted to lay hold on eternal life as a matter of practical experience, and by and by at the coming of our Lord Jesus Christ we shall enter into life eternal in all its fullness.

I have eternal life now in a dying body. In that day body, soul, and spirit will be fully conformed to the image of God's blessed Son. That will be life indeed.

It is a question whether the opening of verse 8 refers to what has already been put before us in verses 4–7 or whether it introduces the words that follow.

If we take it in the latter way, then it balances with 1 Timothy 1:15, where we read, "This is a faithful saying, and worthy of all acceptation, that Christ Jesus came into the world to save sinners." Here we are told, "This is a faithful saying, and these things I will that thou affirm constantly, that they which have believed in God might be careful to maintain good works." All such things as these are good and profitable to men.

But occupation with idle theories is of no value toward a holy life, and so we read: "But avoid foolish questions, and genealogies, and contentions, and strivings about the law; for they are unprofitable and vain." It is easy to give one's self to the defense of certain views which may not in themselves be of a sanctifying character, but the servant of Christ is exhorted to avoid everything of a merely contentious nature, and first of all to have in mind the edification of the people of God.

Verses 10–11 have to do with one who refuses these admonitions. "A man that is an heretic after the first and second admonition reject; knowing that he that is such is subverted, and sinneth, being condemned of himself."

The heretic is really a factious person, more concerned about gathering adherents to himself and maintaining some sectarian view of truth, than falling into line with the entire body of revelation, seeking the blessing of all the people of God. His particular hobby may or may not be true, but he uses it to form a school of opinion.

Such a man is to be shunned after he has been twice admonished to refrain from his behavior. It is the same word as in 1 Timothy 4:7; 5:11; and 2 Timothy 2:23, and in those passages translated "refuse" and "avoid."

There is no hint here of excommunicating the man. False doctrine opposed to fundamental truth is not in question, but the factious man is to be refused; in other words, people are not to listen to him. The result will be, if he persist in his course, that he will eventually go out himself.

The closing verses are all of a personal nature. Paul is about to send either Artemas or Tychicus to Crete to relieve Titus, who is then to come to him at Nicopolis, for there the apostle had made up his mind to winter.

Zenas, the lawyer—possibly a converted Jewish lawyer, that is, a teacher of the law of Moses, or (what seems more likely from his Gentile name) a legal advocate who has become a servant of Christ—and Apollos were evidently also visiting Crete. Titus was exhorted to help them forward in their journey, seeing that they were cared for in temporal things, in order that they might not be left in need.

The saints themselves are exhorted to labor in useful occupations in order to provide for their necessities. This seems to be the true meaning of the admonition. The Christian should shun merely gainful professions or means of livelihood if they are not really "honest trades" for the good of mankind.

Paul and his companions salute Titus, sending their greetings to all who love them in the faith.

The epistle closes with the customary Pauline benediction, "Grace be with you all. Amen."

PART 4

PHILEMON

CHAPTER 1

INTRODUCTION

It has been well said that the letter from Paul to his friend Philemon is the finest specimen of early, personal, Christian correspondence extant. It was written to commend a returning, runaway, thieving slave to his master. With characteristic generosity and a deep sense of the importance of maintaining a standard of righteousness, Paul offers to be surety for this man, Onesimus, and agrees to meet every responsibility as to his past evildoing. He knew that the life of Onesimus had been changed completely by divine grace, and so he unhesitatingly requested Philemon to receive him, no longer as a slave but as a brother in Christ.

Luther said, "We are all God's Onesimi." For in this incident we have a striking picture of our lost condition by nature and practice and of the activities of divine grace on our behalf. The letter sets forth most beautifully the great truths of forgiveness on the ground of the expiatory work of Another and acceptance in the Beloved.

In Philemon himself we have an excellent example of what Christianity could do for one who was, doubtless, a heathen idolater before he was brought to know Christ, but in whom the love of the Spirit was manifested richly after he was brought to a saving knowledge of the Lord Jesus. Apparently, he was converted through the personal ministry of Paul, although the Apostle had never visited Colosse where Philemon resided.

Although so definitely personal, this letter is as truly part of the inspired Word of God as any other portion of the Scriptures. But inspiration leaves room for the writer's personality to manifest itself, and in this intimate epistle we get a wonderful view into the very depths of the Apostle's heart. It is a remarkable thing that so large a part of the New Testament is made up of letters, a form of literature which leaves room for the most simple, homely touches and which stands in vivid contrast to heavy theological treatises. It is as though our God and Father would speak to our hearts in a tender, familiar manner, calculated to win our fullest confidence.

This letter may have been written by Paul while in prison in Cesarea, as some think, but more likely in Rome. Onesimus, a bondman of the household of Philemon, had run away after robbing his master, and, in some way, had come in contact with Paul, through whom he was led to Christ. He felt he should return home to Colosse and submit himself to Philemon, so Paul wrote this letter to explain matters clearly.

Paul was not a recluse. Though in some respects he lived a lonely life for the gospel's sake (1 Cor. 9:5), foregoing the joy and comfort of wife and home that he might be freer to go about preaching the Word, yet he was a man of deep emotions and of very sincere affection. He valued Christian fellowship. He rejoiced when those he loved in Christ labored with acceptance and lived well to the glory of God. He was deeply pained when any turned away and made shipwreck of their discipleship (2 Tim. 4:10). His personal letters show how deep was his interest in others and how fervently he loved his converts and friends. Read carefully this epistle, with these considerations in view, and you will see how true it is.

This letter furnishes us with one of the most delightful pictures of the grace of God, as revealed in the gospel, that we could ever expect to find. Like Onesimus, we have all wronged our rightful Lord and Master. We have misused His mercies, trampled on His grace, and robbed Him by applying for our own selfish purposes that which He has entrusted to us to be used for His honor and glory. But the Lord Jesus has paid all our debt, discharged every obligation to the broken law of God. Now we can come to the Father in His name, assured of a welcome, and knowing we shall not only be forgiven, but also that we are now accepted in the Beloved and brought into the very family of God. It should ever be our happy privilege, as it is our great responsibility, to manifest the same grace to others as that which has been lavished on us.

CHAPTER 2

CHRISTIANITY AND SLAVERY

Philemon 1–25

The spread of Christianity did not drive slavery out of the world all at once. But from the beginning it established a new conception of human values, and Christian masters learned to esteem and treat their slaves as brothers and sisters in Christ. Under Roman law it would not have proved a kindness, in all circumstances, to free the slaves. But as the centuries went on and men became more enlightened, it was through the teachings of Christ and His apostles that slavery disappeared from the civilized world.

But we have stood too long at the door, as it were. Let us enter in and explore the precious things here revealed.

> Paul, a prisoner of Jesus Christ, and Timothy our brother, unto Philemon our dearly beloved, and fellowlabourer, and to our beloved Apphia, and Archippus our fellowsoldier, and to the church in thy house: grace to you, and peace, from God our Father and the Lord Jesus Christ. I thank my God, making mention of thee always in my prayers, hearing of thy love and faith, which thou hast toward the Lord Jesus, and toward all saints; that the communication of thy faith may become effectual by the acknowledging of every good thing which is in you in Christ Jesus. For we have great joy and consolation in thy love, because the bowels of the saints are refreshed by thee, brother. (vv. 1–7)

"A prisoner of Jesus Christ, . . . unto Philemon." This letter was written, in all likelihood, from that hired house in Rome (Acts 28:30) where Paul was kept in durance for two years while he waited to appear before Nero. Philemon was a Colossian believer who owed his conversion to Paul (see v. 19). The letter, as we have mentioned above, concerns the return of a runaway slave. *Paul* means "the little one" and *Philemon,* "the loving one," so this is a letter from the little one to the loving one.

"Apphia . . . Archippus." *Apphia* is a feminine name and refers doubtless to Philemon's wife. *Archippus* was apparently a young preacher, perhaps their son. None can speak with certainty, though, as to this.

"Grace . . . and peace." It is the customary apostolic salutation uniting those of the Gentiles who said "Grace" *(Chans,* or *Gratia)* and the Jews who said "Peace" *(Shalom)* in ordinary greetings. Both are united in Christ.

"Making mention of thee always in my prayers." How real was the interest that the apostle had in this friend and convert! He prayed frequently and regularly for him.

"Hearing of thy love and faith." The two went hand-in-hand. Philemon's genuine Christian character was well-known. Paul rejoiced in the way others spoke of his friend's true piety. Faith works (or, is manifested) by love. Philemon was one to whom the Lord Jesus was precious, and so his heart went out in affection toward all who were in Christ.

"Thy faith . . . effectual by the acknowledging of every good thing which is in you in Christ Jesus." This was not fulsome flattery, but recognition of what the grace of God had wrought in the life and experience of this man. Because of this, Paul felt he could write with confidence as he was about to bring before Philemon the case of Onesimus. He would see every good impulse come to perfection in a practical way. Remember, he was about to plead for a brotherly reception to Onesimus, formerly a thieving, runaway slave.

"Great joy and consolation in thy love." Nothing is more precious than the manifestation of the Spirit of Christ in his people. Philemon's fine, gracious spirit had made him a blessing to many. Now Paul was about to test him further. He adds, "The bowels of the saints are refreshed by thee." For "bowels" we might properly substitute "hearts" in English. The thought is that Philemon's love had cheered the inward being of many a believer.

> Wherefore, though I might be much bold in Christ to enjoin thee that which is convenient, yet for love's sake I rather beseech thee, being such an one as Paul the aged, and now also a prisoner of Jesus Christ.

> I beseech thee for my son Onesimus, whom I have begotten in my bonds: which in time past was to thee unprofitable, but now profitable to thee and to me: whom I have sent again: thou therefore receive him, that is, mine own bowels: whom I would have retained with me, that in thy stead he might have ministered unto me in the bonds of the gospel: but without thy mind would I do nothing; that thy benefit should not be as it were of necessity, but willingly. (vv. 8–14)

"I might be much bold in Christ to enjoin thee that which is convenient." Because of the close tie that bound these two together in Christ and also because of his apostolic authority, Paul might have been free to give a definite commandment as to what would be befitting in the treatment of Onesimus on his return, now that he, too, had become a Christian.

"For love's sake I rather beseech thee." Yet he did not choose to exercise such authority, but preferred to lay the matter before his friend, reminding him that he was now "Paul the aged," in such a way as to give him the opportunity of manifesting that love which ever characterized him, freely, of his own volition and not as acting under stress of any kind.

"I beseech thee for my son Onesimus, whom I have begotten in my bonds." This makes it clear that Onesimus was Paul's child in the faith. He had won him for Christ, and he was naturally concerned as to his future. Where the grace of Christ rules in the heart, *I command* becomes *I beseech.*

"In time past . . . unprofitable, but now profitable." It is a play upon words. *Onesimus* means "profitable" or "helpful." He had been anything but that in the past. Now all was changed, and he was living up to his name. We "are all gone out of the way"; we "are together become unprofitable" (Rom. 3:12) in our sinful condition. It is grace alone that enables those who are saved to count for God.

"Whom I have sent again." Under existing conditions, because of both Roman law and Philemon's character, Paul felt it wisest and best that this slave should return to his master. So, rather than act on the letter of the Mosaic law (Deut. 23:15–16), he sent him back with this letter of commendation.

"Whom I would have retained with me." Paul would have been glad if he had felt free to keep Onesimus with him, as he had proved useful in many ways, and he considered that he might have accepted such service as though it were done by Philemon himself.

"Without thy mind would I do nothing." He would not presume on Philemon's friendship, however, and as there was no opportunity to consult him in the matter, he preferred to have Onesimus return to his former home.

> For perhaps he therefore departed for a season, that thou shouldest receive him for ever; not now as a servant, but above a servant, a brother beloved, specially to me, but how much more unto thee, both in the flesh, and in the Lord? If thou count me therefore a partner, receive him as myself. If he hath wronged thee, or oweth thee ought, put that on mine account; I Paul have written it with mine own hand, I will repay it: albeit I do not say to thee how thou owest unto me even thine own self besides. Yea, brother, let me have joy of thee in the Lord: refresh my bowels in the Lord. Having confidence in thy obedience I wrote unto thee, knowing that thou wilt also do more than I say. (vv. 15–21)

"That thou shouldest receive him for ever." Now that both master and slave were one in Christ, Paul trusted there might be no future rupture of their association, but rather a fellowship on much higher ground than in times past.

"Not now as a servant, but . . . a brother beloved." This gives us to realize what vast changes Christianity was working already in the early church. The one-time slave was now to be recognized as a beloved brother in the Lord. Onesimus in his wayward career pictures the course of all unsaved people. Repentant and truly converted, he goes home to his master. The great doctrine of substitution is illustrated by Paul's offer to pay his debt. The truth of acceptance is suggested when Paul intimates that they are to show their regard for him by the way they treat Onesimus. It is a delightful miniature of the evangel.

"If thou count me therefore a partner, receive him as myself." What a beautiful picture is this of our acceptance in Christ! In the case of every saved sinner it is as though our Lord presents him to the Father saying, "If Thou count Me as a Partner, receive him as Myself." We "are complete in him" (Col. 2:10), for, "As he is, so are we in this world" (1 John 4:17). He says to the Father, "Thou . . . hast loved them, [even] as thou hast loved me" (John 17:23). How foolish Onesimus would have been if he had thrown away Paul's letter and undertaken to plead his own case! There can be no greater folly than to ignore the mediatorial work of Christ and seek to approach God in one's own fancied merit.

"If he . . . oweth thee aught, put that on mine account." It is evident that Onesimus had robbed his master. Paul offers to settle everything for him even as our blessed Lord paid all our debt upon the cross that we might be justified from all things.

"Thou owest unto me even thine own self besides." Delicately, Paul reminds Philemon that it was through him that Philemon had been brought to know Christ. Thus Paul felt sure he could count on Philemon acting now in accordance with his wishes.

"Let me have joy of thee in the Lord." Loving compliance with the Apostle's request on the part of Philemon would gladden the heart of him who was a prisoner for the sake of Christ's name. When one has been saved by grace, it is to be expected that he will walk in grace toward others, even to those whom he feels have mistreated and deceived him.

"Knowing that thou wilt also do more than I say." Not for a moment did Paul doubt but that Philemon would do that which had been asked of him. He did this with the full assurance in his own heart that he would not be disappointed, but that Philemon would go even beyond what was requested in true Christian charity and brotherliness. So the letter was committed to Onesimus, who wended his way back to Colosse, assured that all would be forgiven and his would be a new standing altogether in the household of his former master.

> But withal prepare me also a lodging: for I trust that through your prayers I shall be given unto you. There salute thee Epaphras, my fellowprisoner in Christ Jesus; Marcus, Aristarchus, Demas, Lucas, my fellowlabourers. The grace of our Lord Jesus Christ be with your spirit. Amen. (vv. 22–25)

"Through your prayers." Paul confidently expected his acquittal, and believed he would be free again to visit his friends and minister among them. He counted on God answering the prayers of many on his behalf. Nor was he disappointed, for according to the most authentic records that have come down to us, he was set free when he appeared before Nero and permitted to labor on in the gospel for several years before he was rearrested. He was then taken again to Rome, where he was incarcerated in the Mamertine dungeon, and after official condemnation he was beheaded as a martyr for the gospel of Christ.

"Epaphras, my fellowprisoner." This was the man of God who had come to Paul from Colosse, bringing an account of the love of the saints and also of the efforts of certain teachers of evil doctrine to pervert this young church (see Col. 1:7–8; 4:12). He seems to have shared Paul's imprisonment for a time at least, whether voluntarily or otherwise we are not told.

"My fellowlabourers." The four names mentioned are all of real interest. Mark was the relative of Barnabas, whom Paul refused to take on his second missionary journey, but who went with Barnabas when the two older men separated. In the years that followed he had lived down his early lack of reliability, and Paul now valued his fellowship and testimony (see 2 Tim. 4:11).

Aristarchus was a devoted friend to Paul, and at this time he was also a fellow prisoner with him (Col. 4:10). The names of Demas and Luke, the beloved physician, are here linked together, as also in Colossians 4:14. Alas, later on they were separated because of Demas' defection. He forsook Paul the prisoner because he loved this present world (2 Tim. 4:10).

"The grace of our Lord Jesus Christ be with you." It is the customary Pauline salutation, emphasizing the grace whereby alone we are saved, and which was the distinguishing mark that authenticated all the Apostle's genuine letters.

Paul's personal correspondence was the outcome of a heart devoted to Christ. What of our letters? Do we seek to help others to know Him better as we write?